Abraham Friesen
Dept. of History
University of California
Santa Barbara

Marxism and Radical Religion

ESSAYS TOWARD A
REVOLUTIONARY HUMANISM
*Edited by John C. Raines
and Thomas Dean*

*Temple University Press
Philadelphia   1970*

Standard Book Number 87722–002–6
Library of Congress Card Number 78–119903
Printed in the United States of America
Copyright © by Temple University
Philadelphia — 19122

CONTENTS

To be radical is to grasp things by the root.
But for man the root is man himself.

KARL MARX, *Critique of Hegel's* Philosophy of Right

NOTES ON CONTRIBUTORS

HERBERT MARCUSE is a professor of philosophy at the University of California (San Diego) and formerly taught for many years at Brandeis University. A prominent Marxist theoretician and philosopher of the New Left, he is the author of many books, including *Reason and Revolution*, *Eros and Civilization*, *One-Dimensional Man*, and *An Essay on Liberation*.

JAN M. LOCHMAN is a professor of theology at the Comenius Faculty in Prague, Czechoslovakia, and is currently on the theological faculty at the University of Basel, Switzerland. An active member of the World Council of Churches, he is known to American readers through his articles on "Ecumenical Theology of Revolution" in *New Theology No. 6*, edited by M. Marty and D. G. Peerman (New York, 1969) and "The Church and the Humanization of Society," *Union Seminary Quarterly Review* (1969).

RICHARD SHAULL, who for many years was active in Colombia and Brazil in the church's work for social change, is now professor of ecumenics at Princeton Theological Seminary. One of the leading exponents in the World Council of Churches of a theology of revolution, he is the author of several articles and books, including *Encounter with Revolution* and (with Carl Oglesby) *Containment and Change*.

JOHN C. BENNETT is president of Union Theological Seminary in New York City and professor of Christian ethics. He is the author of numerous books and articles, including *Christians and the State* and *Christianity and Communism Today*.

FRANKLIN H. LITTELL is a professor of religion at Temple University and author of many books and articles, including *Church and the Body Politic* and *Wild Tongues: A Handbook of Social Pathology*.

JOHN C. RAINES is an assistant professor of religion at Temple University and author of "Sin as Pride and Sin as Sloth: Reinhold Niebuhr and Karl Marx on Man's Predicament," *Christianity and Crisis* (February 1969).

PAUL M. VAN BUREN is a professor of religion at Temple University and the author of *The Secular Meaning of the Gospel* and a more recent collection of essays, *Theological Explorations*.

THOMAS DEAN is an assistant professor of religion at Temple University and author of "Heidegger, Marx and Secular Theology," *Union Seminary Quarterly Review* (1967).

INTRODUCTION

This book grows out of a two-day conference on "Marxism, Religion, and the Liberal Tradition" held at Temple University in April 1969 under the sponsorship of the department of religion. The aim of the conference, and of this collection of essays based upon it, has been to bring together liberals and radicals, Christians and Marxists, religious and secular thinkers, to consider the new radical perspective emerging in American society today. As was noted at the outset of the conference, Marxism and religion are each the name of an establishment and of a rebellion against an establishment in the name of man. These essays are concerned to explore ways in which a revolutionary humanism can draw upon Marxist and Christian insights to criticize existing doctrines and institutions and to shape its own vision of a more human future.

The historical circumstances and motives underlying current revolutionary movements are well known. In every part of the world, the inner contradictions of immense economic, technological, and social forces have given rise to struggles within and against the established order. Student protests in America and Asia against the neo-colonial and imperialist policies of corporate capitalism have been paralleled in Eastern Europe by demonstrations against bureaucratic state power in the name of a more democratic socialism. Revolutionary movements for national liberation in the third-world nations of Asia, Africa, and Latin America have been joined by the revolt of black, Spanish-speaking, and Indian Americans at home. It has been said that revolution is the dominant salvation myth of our time. But it is more. To many, it has become the major *practical* vehicle of men's hopes.

For religion, in particular for religion in America, this revolutionary humanism poses a direct challenge to those who would remove social ("secular") concerns from the private sanctuary of piety and belief. But, of course, liberal religion and the social gospel have already fought that battle. In more radical quarters, there is a further conviction that this traditional problem of "the relation of religion to society" is no longer valid. The issue may retain a rearguard interest or fascination, but religion, even radical religion, on this reading, no longer constitutes the cutting edge of man's future. Still others hold that it is too early to predict with confidence the development of religion beyond its contemporary crisis: whether religion will prove capable and important in supporting man's quest for a more human world remains, for them, an open question.

For Marxists, on the other hand, this revolutionary humanism threatens to subvert the original historical depository and chief engine of the orthodox revolutionary tradition. If institutional religion is today viewed by many of its former adherents as irrelevant to the concrete humanization of society, institutionalized Marxism, as typified by the Soviet state, is likewise coming to be viewed by some Marxist thinkers and in some socialist states as a major (though not the chief) reactionary force blocking the path to a more genuine socialist humanism. Advocates of a movement of critical renewal within the Marxist tradition, these thinkers offer a radically new Marxist-humanist analysis of the revolutionary possibilities of post-industrial society and look not to older European traditions but to more recent third-world experiences for their models of revolutionary *praxis*.[1]

These changing circumstances have resulted in unexpected alignments within both the forces of the establishment and the forces of protest and revolt. Radicals in all camps have been driven together by their common opposition to the forces of the status quo, the established bureaucracies, the professional managers, the wealthy and the powerful, and a "realism" that passes as political wisdom. They have closed ranks in a common realization that the task of their generation is to move beyond the polemics of the cold war, not by indulging in the privileged illusions of "dialogue" and "coexistence," but by inaugurating a new era of practical collaboration or "pro-existence" on behalf of the future of man.[2] Hence, there has arisen around the world a "new left" representing a "third way" that cuts across the established boundaries of religion and secularity, of liberal and socialist societies, of have and have-not nations, a left which as yet has no official doctrine or institutional status, but which has committed itself to the revolutionary realization of what it considers an increasingly realistic "utopian" vision of man.

It is Marx's early writings which have provided radical

1. For a helpful description of these new Marxist humanists, see Rosemary Reuther, "The New Left: Revolutionaries after the Fall of the Revolution," *Soundings*, LII:3 (Fall 1969), pp. 245–263.
2. The term "pro-existence" and its significance for the rapprochement of Marxist and Christian radicals are discussed in the introduction to *The Christian Marxist Dialogue*, edited by Paul Oestreicher (New York, 1969), pp. 1–29.

humanists with the categories, spiritual and material, for their revolutionary assault upon liberalism and orthodox Marxism alike. Marx's original vision, long regarded as peculiar or "foreign" to the western liberal tradition, principally because it was reduced to "nothing but" a precursor of Stalinist terror, has come to be seen by radical thinkers as what Marx himself always maintained it to be — the most authentic expression of the radical libertarian values of western social thought. Moreover, those features of orthodox Marxism which have received the most serious criticism now appear to be rooted in the negative aspects of that same western tradition.[3] In both instances, the example of the young Marx has freed contemporary radicals to "resecularize" or humanize the Marxist-socialist tradition.

Radical Christians have traditionally derived their social categories from the central prophetic and eschatological elements of biblical faith. But they, too, have been freed by the new revolutionary humanism to appropriate what Herbert Marcuse calls the "radical heretic" tradition — those apocalyptic and revolutionary elements in western church history which for a long time were only marginally significant but which in the left wing of the Reformation and again in our own day have emerged as a dynamic "third force" over against the "Constantinian" establishments of Protestantism and Catholicism. It thus becomes possible to suggest a variety of ways in which Christians who find themselves moving toward a clearer and firmer commitment to a revolutionary humanism can come to a better understanding of themselves as in some sense both radicals and Christians.

The essays in the first half of this volume introduce some of the issues raised by radical humanists within and over against the establishments of Marxist and liberal societies.

3. For a collection of essays reinterpreting Marx's relationship to the western liberal tradition, see *Marx and the Western World*, edited by Nicholas Lobkowicz (Notre Dame, Indiana, 1967).

Herbert Marcuse defends Marxism's revolutionary break with the liberal-bourgeois embodiment of western radical libertarian values, but criticizes the existing socialist states for their failure to carry this revolution through. From a creative reinterpretation of original Marxism he derives the model of a qualitatively new man and guidelines for a society based upon it. *Jan Lochman* describes the temporary coming together of Marxism, liberalism, and religion in the remarkable events of 1968 in Czechoslovakia. An entire nation rose up against the state's claim to absolute power and truth and, inspired by its heritage of democratic freedom and religious hope, bore witness to an alternative vision of a "socialism with a human face." The fact that this essay was originally presented on the very eve of Premier Dubček's removal from political authority adds a particular depth and humanity to its concluding pages.

Turning to the American scene, *Richard Shaull* argues that effective criticism of American society today requires political and social remedies of the radical sort being used in Latin America. He finds in the biblical faith a revolutionary perspective and models for the formation of "radical communities" in which that perspective can become operative. In reply, *John Bennett* acknowledges the need, in light of the new radical criticism, for a revision of religious liberalism and Niebuhrian realism, points out the contribution of the churches to the contextual and theological arguments for revolutionary violence, and calls Christian radicals to work for revolutionary social change within the framework of "a new liberal-radical politics."

The essays in the second part of the volume place this contemporary movement toward radical religion in historical, sociological, philosophical, and theological perspective. *Franklin Littell* points to the historical precedents and resources in the left-wing Reformation for a radical view on contemporary society: the Puritan "agitators'" initiation of anti-establishmentarian struggles for religious liberty, voluntary association, and participatory democracy; the occurrence in Thomas Münzer of a dramatic fusion of radical religion and revolutionary politics. *John Raines* argues that this shift from passive to active man became explicit only with Marx's radical reinterpretation of man as the sole creator of his human (social, historical) world. As Raines describes them, the revolutionary implications of this shift in self-consciousness are still not realized either in contemporary American society or by those who adhere to the traditional insights of biblical faith.

Paul van Buren analyzes the peculiar situation of Christians who are both political and theological radicals. Partially alienated from the biblical tradition, open to the experiences of modern, secular men, Christian radicals nevertheless continue to tell the original Christian story. But now it is told as a non-theistic story about men. Through its guiding images and metaphors, it speaks to men's questions about the human "story" (history) itself. In the final essay, *Thomas Dean* criticizes the arguments and presuppositions of radically secular theology. Such theology succeeds only by adopting certain independent insights of secular thought which prove to be inconsistent with its theological starting point. As theology, it is compromised also in its ability to translate its imaginative vision into practical forces for "changing the world." A radical perspective requires instead a new humanistic metaphysics.

Enough has been said to indicate that the reader will not find detailed or even very general agreement among these essays. The most basic divergence of opinion occurs not between Marxists and Christians (who are sometimes one and the same person) but between those of a liberal or establishmentarian persuasion and those of a radical anti-establishmentarian attitude. This division is reflected in disagreement over such catchwords as "revolution" versus "reform," or again, over the temporal coefficient of social

change. For some of the contributors, that temporal perspective has been radically foreshortened, so that apocalyptic
or utopian images have advanced from speculative possibility
to realistic necessity. For others, the appeal to reasoned dissent and the militant use of legitimate, that is, officially sanctioned or non-violent means of change, have not been fully
exhausted and are, at least in the non-revolutionary situations,
the only effective method for rapid social change.

The essayists disagree also on the religious implications of
this secular dilemma. Does the Christian tradition, radically
understood, support these new utopias, or does it, like conventional political wisdom, scale them down to the less dramatic but more manageable proportions of, in Martin Marty's
phrase, "usable futures"? Is it true, as sometimes alleged, that
radical humanists, if not Marx himself, live off the spiritual
capital of the Judeo-Christian tradition without reinvesting
in it, or is precisely the opposite the case? If Christians come
to view the problems of contemporary America in ways that
significantly resemble the original Marxist critique, what
must they conclude as Americans and as Christians?

Much has been omitted for reasons of space or focus that
could usefully have been included in this collection — in particular, religious views other than Protestant or Christian. It
can be argued, however, that the views which are represented
have a wider application. To give a practical example, recent
meetings of the World Council of Churches indicate that the
task of the churches today is no longer to compare different
religious views or to offer religious alternatives to secular
views. Rather, it is to bring their resources to bear upon the
actual, worldly conditions of men, "to change all the conditions under which man is an oppressed, enslaved, destitute
and despised being." Religion is discovering the truth of
Marx's thesis that differences among competing views of the
world, be they secular or religious, are irrelevant (or worse)
except as they change the world. But this criterion of praxis
brings out in all religions the same basic polarities of response

to be found in this volume. Therefore, the views represented have relevance beyond Protestant Christianity or the American scene.

American religious thinkers are beginning to identify with the effort of a new generation to construct a theoretical framework for a revolutionary humanism and a radical perspective on society. This book is evidence of that fact. Whether Christianity is capable of contributing to that effort by becoming a more "material" religion, as radical Christians claim, is not yet clear. Perhaps radical religion itself will be so transformed as to be indistinguishable from a secular faith. In the end, these questions cannot be settled by thought alone. What matters is that such thinking be continually tested by its capacity to extend man's freedom and make it real. For a radical perspective, as Marx said, the root is man.

In concluding, we should like to thank the many persons who worked to make the original conference and this volume possible: first of all, Bernard Phillips, chairman of the department of religion at Temple University, without whose counsel and support our projects would never have been realized; our colleagues and staff in the department of religion for their participation in the work of the conference and their advice on the book — in particular, Robert Gordis, Paul van Buren, Elwyn Smith, Samuel Laeuchli, and Hazel Topham, who chaired meetings or in other ways contributed to the success of the conference; our colleagues in other departments for lending their presence and efforts to our meetings; and, finally, the staff of Temple University Press for their considerable help in bringing the results of our conference before the public. It remains only to add that none of these persons should be held responsible for the editors' decisions concerning the final form and content of these essays.

JOHN C. RAINES

THOMAS DEAN

1 *Marxism, Religion, and the Liberal Tradition*

MARXISM AND THE NEW HUMANITY: AN UNFINISHED REVOLUTION

Herbert Marcuse

In the context of the contemporary situation, and with the special emphasis on the present student movement, what is the relationship between Marxism and the western tradition? Marxism itself once defined, relatively simply, its relationship to the liberal tradition and its place in it. Marxism claimed, namely, to translate the progressive ideas of liberalism into reality, to take them out of the sphere of mere values (professed but rarely practiced), out of the entire ideological sphere, and to make the concepts of freedom, equality, and justice for all *real*. Marx considered this translation of liberal ideas into reality impossible under the social system from which liberalism had emerged and with which liberalism remained connected: capitalism.

Within capitalist society, the liberal ideas of freedom, equality, and justice remain abstract and ideological. This is so because in such a society the great majority of people remain dependent on the class owning and controlling the process of production, a class whose very rule is based on the continuation of this control. There is, therefore, underlying this system, a factual, basic inequality within the system itself that cannot be eliminated, and it is this factual and basic inequality that vitiates the progressive ideas of liberalism and leads to an increasing restriction of their substance and function.

Without dwelling on the way in which Marx demonstrated this thesis, it can be recalled that Marx accepted the idea of freedom as self-determination and of democracy as the form of government of a free society. But the existing society is not free; therefore, an authentic democracy does not exist and cannot prevail in this society. In addition, Marx considered civil rights and liberties an essential part of democracy but, unless implemented in an economic democracy, freedom, equality, and justice would remain privileges, and popular sovereignty an illusion. Marx broke with the liberal tradition by insisting that only a revolution could establish real freedom, equality, and justice.

AN UNFINISHED REVOLUTION

However it appears today that this break with the liberal tradition is incomplete, and that the ways of translating liberal ideas into reality are no longer those envisaged by Marx. Today, for example, it can be seen that existing socialist societies succumb to repressive forces within their own system. It appears that these repressive tendencies are not due merely to the fact of coexistence, to competition with capitalism, but that there is something in the basic Marxian concept itself which seems to justify the extension of repressive tendencies from the old societies to the new. It also appears that the present rebellion of militant youth is directed largely against this intrusion of the old into the new society. Or, to put it another way, this rebellion invokes neglected goals and ideas, invokes forgotten liberating and libertarian forces in Marxian theory itself.

It may be noted that this opposition to Marxism among the New Left often appears as a return from the mature to the early Marx. Really radical and revolutionary ideas are to be found much more in the early Marx than in Das Kapital, so that a reading today of early Marxist writings reveals not a soft Marxian humanism but rather a truly and authentically radical concept.

The ingress of the old society into the new provides a continuity rooted in the concept of reason which underlies the Marxian theory — a concept that still pays tribute to the rationality of scarcity and domination. In what way? The key is found in the notion "development of the productive forces." The socialist society is characterized by a rational, unfettered development of the productive forces, a development which, under capitalism, is becoming more and more repressive and destructive.

It is this notion of the development of the productive forces which extends the past into the future. This is clearly revealed in Marx's distinction between the two phases in the construction of socialism: the phase of creation of economic equality, and the phase of creation of the society beyond necessity. According to this concept, the new socialist society is supposed, in the first phase, to create the material conditions for freedom and equality, the material conditions for implementation of the socialist principle "to each according to his needs." Vast social wealth would obviously be required to translate this ideal "to each according to his needs" into reality. During the period of creation of this wealth, during the creation of the material conditions for freedom, repression would continue, inequality would continue, because society would not yet be rich enough to afford socialism.

The dangers of this concept of the two phases are known today. For one thing, the first phase, especially under prevailing international conditions, could apparently be pro-

longed indefinitely. But there is more to it than that. Even
in the fully developed socialist society, Marx assumed, there
is one area in which there cannot be real freedom: the area
of socially necessary work, socially necessary labor. The famous formulation in the third volume of *Das Kapital* is evidence of this. According to that formulation there can be
no freedom in this realm; it remains a realm of necessity.

Technical progress is a prerequisite for the progressive
reduction of the working day; this, and the collective control
of the productive forces by the producers themselves, would
essentially change the character of work, but would remain
beyond and outside the realm of necessity, beyond and outside the realm of socially necessary work.

There is a technological continuity between capitalism and
socialism. The socialist society presupposes the largest possible
automation of labor and the scientific computation of material resources available for the satisfaction of needs. While
socialism destroys the political apparatus of capitalism, it
takes over (and it has to take over) in order to be able to
develop the productive forces, the technical and technological
apparatus whose construction has been the great historic
achievement of capitalism, and without which no free society
is imaginable.

There is, however, one hitch in this thinking. Today it
becomes constantly clearer that the technological apparatus
of production, distribution, and consumption is by no means
a technical, scientific, and technological apparatus only, but
that it is increasingly the apparatus of political control, as
well. And since it is working as apparatus of political control,
it contributes to the achievement of late capitalism in the
most advanced industrial countries — namely, to reconcile
and integrate into the capitalist system precisely those social
classes in which Marx saw the agent, the historic subject of
revolution: the industrial working classes.

Under the impact of the overwhelming productivity of
capitalism and its ability to raise the standard of living, the

very class that was supposed to be free for the revolution (because it had no vested interests in the existing system) has, in the most advanced industrial countries, developed such vested interest. So long as this development continues, the industrial working class is without that quality and qualification which Marx considered an absolutely necessary factor of revolution.

A NEW TYPE OF MAN

Since we are again confronted with a repressed or minimized element in Marxian theory, a succinct restatement of this theory is in order. The industrial working class, according to Marx, is the historic agent of revolution, not only because it constitutes the human basis of the process of production, but also because it is free from the competitive and aggressive needs generated by the capitalist system and satisfied in that system. In other words, the proletariat, according to Marx, is a class that, in this sense, is already free prior to its liberation; and it is this freedom from the satisfactions of the capitalist system which makes it the historic subject of revolution. This idea implies that socialism represents a qualitatively different society, oné which can never be a mere by-product of new institutions and relationships, no matter how basic. The development of socialist institutions and relationships requires, rather, a new type of man, a different type of human being, with new needs, capable of finding a qualitatively different way of life, and of constructing a qualitatively different environment. Unless socialism is built by such a new type of human being, the transition from capitalism to socialism would mean only replacing one form of domination by another form of domination, perhaps more efficient, perhaps even more egalitarian than the capitalist controls (and this of itself would be a great contribution). But by no means would this yet be the qualitatively different life, the life of authentic freedom, that Marx envisaged as the substance of socialism.

If this often forgotten idea, this insistence on a new type of human being as prerequisite to the transition to socialism, is reexamined, the radical libertarian trend in Marxian theory must be recognized. This trend is telescoped in the concept of the "all-around individual." Marx explained this concept by another difficult, strange, and provocative term. He spoke of "the sensuous species being of man." "Sensuous species being" — a type of man who fulfills the potentialities of the human species not only in and with his mental faculties but also in and with his senses, in his sensibility and sensitivity. And among these potentialities of man as species being is precisely the capability of transforming his environment, his world, into a universe where his sensibility can freely develop. This would be a peaceful universe, a universe to be enjoyed.

This means, according to Marx, that the construction of a socialist society is a *creation* rather than a production, a creation expressing and activating not only man's rationality, not only his vital material needs, but all his senses, his reason, his imagination. In the same period and in the same work from which the description of the sensuous species being is quoted, *The Economic-Philosophical Manuscripts*, there is another note by Marx which sounds very strange indeed to our ears and which is a comment rarely noticed. In discussing the broad outline of a socialist society as a creation in the literal sense, Marx stated that man not only produces in accordance with his vital needs, he also produces "in accordance with the laws of beauty."

Here is a vision of socialism as a society where the realm of freedom would not lie beyond and outside the realm of necessary labor. There would be, rather, an entrance of freedom into the realm of necessity, so that rational organization of the process of production would respond to and shape the sensibility of man without twisting it to the demands of exploitation. This would mean development of the productive forces, indeed, but a development directed toward the goal of taking man out of the material process of production, making him the supervisor, the experimenter with the technique and technology of production. It would mean directing the process of production first toward the abolition of poverty and toil the globe over, and then toward the total reconstruction of the spiritually and physically polluted environment of capitalist society.

This vision of a socialist society in which a different type of human being will have emerged, a man with a new sensibility and sensitivity, physiologically incapable of tolerating an ugly, noisy, and polluted universe — this is the radical libertarian element in Marxian theory, an element so often concealed by the rationalistic (and today already largely obsolescent) emphasis on the perpetual growth of productivity and production.

In other words, the relationship between capitalism and socialism indicates not only an economic rupture, not only a political rupture, and not merely an ascending curve of development of productive forces, but, in addition to this, an essential *redirection* of the process of production, redirection toward the goals just indicated. For the technically most highly developed (even overdeveloped) capitalist countries, that would mean perhaps not further development of the productive forces but rather their retrenchment according to goals requiring the elimination of the waste and planned obsolescence which this system retains — both abroad and at home — in the face of misery, hunger, and oppression. It would indeed mean (and I think we should be frank about this) a reduction in the standard of living, but a reduction in the standard of living for those who live on profitable waste, luxury, and destruction.

MARXISM AND RADICAL RELIGION

This libertarian radicalism seems to link Marxism with a quite different western tradition. This would be not so much the liberal tradition (which still contains much of the repressive puritanism with which it was once connected), but the great radical heretic movements which, since the twelfth and thirteenth centuries, have become an essential element in the western tradition: libertarian trends in Christianity, libertarian humanism, Brothers of the Free Spirit, Edomites, and others.

While Marxian theory remains irreconcilable with Christian dogma and its institution, it finds an ally in those tendencies, groups, and individuals committed to the part of the Christian teaching that stands uncompromisingly against inhuman, exploitative power. In our times these radical religious tendencies have come to life in the priests and ministers who have joined the struggle against fascism in all its forms, and those who have made common cause with the liberation movements in the Third World, especially in Latin America. They are part of the global anti-authoritarian movement against the self-perpetuating power structure, east and west, which is less and less interested in human progress. This anti-authoritarian character brings to life long-forgotten or reduced anarchist, heretic tendencies.

Even the bizarre, extreme forms which the student opposition assumes today must be taken very seriously. They express, it seems, the fact that the young militants have lost patience with the traditional forms of opposition which go on and on without really changing the essentials — which go on and on, still sustaining the ghettoes, still sustaining and even extending poverty and misery — which still go on while hundreds are daily killed, tortured, and burned in an immoral and illegal war. Whether we like it or not, this opposition exists.

This brings us full circle. There is indeed a force in this opposition with which religion and the churches should properly come to grips, because there is a strong moral element in it, a moral element which has for too long been neglected or overlooked. This moral element has now become a political force.

MARXISM, LIBERALISM, AND RELIGION: AN EAST EUROPEAN PERSPECTIVE

Jan M. Lochman

The question of the relationship among the Marxist, liberal, and religious traditions emerged with unexpected urgency in Czechoslovakia in 1968. We can say with unexpected urgency because five — or even three — years ago such a problem would have seemed purely academic. Of that trinity of subjects — Marxism, liberalism, and religion — one member was nearly dead. To many, political liberalism was not destroyed in our country in 1948; it had already been destroyed in the deadly crisis of European liberalism in 1938. The Munich agreement, in which the western liberal democracies sold out a liberal democratic Czechoslovakia to fascism, was a mortal blow to the once cherished liberal tradition. Thus, liberalism was practically dead from that time on. The other member of that trinity, religion, also seemed pretty much dying — still alive, to be sure, but more or less on the margins of society. Thus, in our culture we moved (to speak in theological terms) from a "trinitarian" cultural pattern to a unitarian pattern. Marxism was the only official political and cultural power left.

Then came the year 1968. It raised all over again the question of the relationship of these three members, and on a new level (this is important to emphasize). There was now no attempt to go back; rather, there was the question of the future of our own socialist society, the question of a new orientation to that society. The context in which this new urgency was presented was the radical and perhaps classical political problem: the problem of the humanization of social life. It was not by chance that the matter arose exactly in this context, because here indeed, if anywhere, is a meaningful common ground among the partners of the trinity: Marxism, liberalism (or democracy, preferably), and religion. This common ground is, of course, not very broad. The three traditions differ markedly in their basic concepts. For instance, they give distinctively different answers to the question of what it is to be human, of what humanization means. There can be, therefore, no cheap or easy fusion among the three traditions.

Yet, with all their differences, these three movements agree at least in emphasizing the common direction to their search. They agree that this is the goal of political responsibility and participation: to foster the humanization of our common life, "to change all the conditions under which man is an oppressed, enslaved, destitute, and despised being." This is a sentence from Karl Marx, but it could as well have been uttered from the point of view of the biblical, prophetic heritage, or even from some of the best insights of the liberal tradition. All three movements strive to change those conditions which dehumanize man's common life. And in this understanding of the final goal of political action our three traditions differ clearly from other political perspectives —

especially from those of European and American right-wing movements.

Consequently, it is not by chance that the problem of the relationship among Marxism, religion, and the liberal tradition arose in Czechoslovakia precisely within the context of the Czechoslovak people's effort to humanize their socialist society. With reference to this subject, three aspects of that effort which surfaced in 1968 deserve attention: the three basic concepts of socialism, democracy, and the religious perspective.

THE DEVELOPMENT OF SOCIALISM

The concern for humanization in the Czech society should be understood as a vindication of basic socialist insights and as the logical development of a *socialist* society. This fact is important to recognize. "Socialism with a human face" — this slogan coined by Alexander Dubček became a rallying cry for the overwhelming majority of the people. In this regard, the word socialism should be stressed. There was no mandatory lip service. There was a clear recognition that some of the basic changes achieved by a Marxist society contributed in important ways to the humanization of social conditions.

This becomes clear if these changes are thought about in the light of that sentence of Marx describing humanization as an attempt to change all the conditions under which man is a despised and oppressed being. If this is used as a kind of standard, which is then applied to the Czech society, we surely must acknowledge that some of the most dehumanizing conditions have been effectively changed since 1948. Some of the great social needs of men have been supplied. Let us look at some of them. They are, perhaps, rather rudimentary, but extremely important to human existence.

First, there is no problem of poverty in the Czech society. There is no bitter poverty in the absolute sense. That means there is no one really hungry or undernourished. What is perhaps more important, there is no acute problem of relative poverty such as exists in some of the richest countries of the world — even in the United States, for example. There are no great contrasts between the relatively rich and the relatively poor. The difference in economic status of various groups and individuals in Czech society is small. In this sense, the Czechs are on the way to becoming in reality what is called "a classless society." The status of the traditional, so-called lower classes — for example, of the working class — has lifted considerably; and this is an important moral and psychological phenomenon of humanization.

This can be seen in one of the most inspiring developments of 1968. The working class in Czechoslovakia became actively involved in the goals of democratization and humanization. This did not come about just by chance. There were structural reasons, having to do with the growth of the worker's consciousness. Because of the revolutionary nationalization of Czechoslovakian industry, the workers became the "owners" of a decisive share of the national economy. At the same time, official ideology and propaganda emphasized their leading role in society. They were publicly declared the ruling power of all the national life, the nation's sovereign subjects — no longer to be considered mere "objects." Within the framework of rigid Stalinism this remained truer in theory than in actual practice, to be sure. Yet the theory itself was important. If a socialist society is to be a worker's society, then the workers are bound to become deeply interested in developing its full possibilities, particularly with respect to their own creative social participation as fully responsible subjects of the political process. This theoretic demand took hold in a qualitatively new way in 1968. After certain hesitations in the first weeks, the factories became important central strongholds for the movement of democratization in its endeavor to enhance active participation by all citizens in social decision-making. The unity between the workers and the intelligentsia, particularly the students, became one of the most promising features of that process, and of a dynamic socialism in general.

More of such positive and humanizing phenomena could be mentioned: the national health service and its far-reaching and generous medical care unconditionally at the disposal of all the citizens; or the educational system, open to everyone and free of charge on all its levels. These are, if you wish, everyday phenomena, but in exactly that way, extremely important. In turn, these phenomena are connected to the basic structural change of the economy. This revolutionary process has always had its problems and dangers, and they should be spoken about quite openly. But fundamentally the revolution and the evolution of our society must be considered important steps *forward* in the process of humanizing a relatively developed society.

THE DEMOCRATIC HERITAGE

The assessment of socialism as a positive vehicle for the humanization of a relatively developed society does not indicate that the establishment of a socialist order brings an automatic solution to all problems. The establishment of a socialist society certainly does not mean the realization of a perfect society, to say nothing of the Kingdom of God on earth. The problem of humanization is not solved in all its aspects by the establishment of socialism. On the contrary, socialism poses some new and rather serious questions. If that standard of Marx, the "middle axiom" of humanization, is applied, it must be conceded that not all the conditions under which man is an oppressed, destitute, despised being have been completely overcome by socialism. There remain general elements of alienation which a socialist shares with other types of developed societies. It is even necessary to admit that some new and serious dehumanizing elements emerge in the very process of socialist revolution and evolution.

The most important of these might be described as a certain tendency toward a monopoly of power (political power), and toward a monopoly of truth. It is not the intention here to pass quick moral and religious judgments on these tendencies. That would be too simple. In a sense, the tendency toward this monopoly is historically understandable. A revolutionary change of such depth, the breaking of the economic and social power of the "*ancien regime*," is hardly possible without the radical overthrow of the structures of the preceding social order. The Marxist idea of a dictatorship of the proletariat cannot be *a priori* condemned if socialism is accepted as a step forward on the path to humanization. No one can moralize about this. In all probability it is a necessity of the post-revolutionary order in its first stage.

The danger of such a post-revolutionary order, however, is that it does not discern the signs of the times-*in-time*. That means that it is tempted to eternalize its monopoly and to prolong it beyond the point of possible justification — that is, beyond the stage of achievement of a firmly established socialist system.

This is of course an extremely difficult problem. Biblical anthropology with its deep insight into the strategies of human selfishness and lust for power should make man very sober and unbiased. No wonder many socialist countries, including Czechoslovakia, have found it difficult to resist this trend. Rigid Stalinism became its very incarnation. The "cult of personality" can be spoken of with some justification, because a monopoly of power in the hands of one omnipotent man or group and the monopoly of truth in one omniscient authority were really the outcome, the end, the consequence of that development. Under such circumstances, then, not all the conditions under which man is an oppressed being have been overcome. The question of humanizing the social and political process remains a burning issue.

This problem has an intellectual side. As Dr. Marcuse has pointed out in his essay, there is a certain rationalistic background within Marxism, inherited from the old German idealistic tradition that culminated in Hegel. A certain tendency toward dogmatism, typical especially of Stalinist thought and practice, is meant by this. How often an "orthodox idea" was recklessly imposed on facts and social reality! How often any "deviation" from the official image was severely reprimanded! This attitude blocked the possibility of a continuing progressive movement to change historical situations. It was this "idealism" within the Marxist tradition which was more dangerous than its classical "materialism."

This idealistic rationalism led to a conception of history as a rationally determined process and to a conception of human freedom as recognized necessity. This is not, strictly speaking, an original Marxian concept. Rather, it was taken over from Hegel. To Hegel, history is fundamentally the movement of reason. The moment that one recognizes this "reason," one becomes the master of history. History is in this sense the extension and extrapolation of reason; so that if you have the right philosophy, then you possess all the solutions. That's the danger. The development of Marxism from the young Marx to the old Marx, and from Marx to Engels, Lenin, and Stalin, shows this Hegelian tendency: freedom is recognized necessity.

But there is another trend in Marxism, one that is to be taken very seriously. By this is meant the original attitude of Karl Marx himself. This attitude questions the inherited deterministic concept of history. Marx's starting point was a philosophy of *praxis*. *Praxis* means that one does not have all the solutions, so to say, beforehand. In acting, man creates a new reality, new conditions, by that action. This philosophy of *praxis* was always then a classical Marxist idea. It checked the temptation of rationalistic determinism. Thus Marxism always had some "built-in" possibilities of disenchanting fa-

talistic conceptions of history. It always had certain resources
for rethinking the situation, reacting to new conditions, acting responsively.

The great contribution of Marxism probably lies exactly
here, in its basic dialectic. Marxism is neither irrationalistic —
because it sees certain patterns of development and takes
them seriously — nor is it rationalistic in the Hegelian sense,
because it emphasizes the creative possibilities for action.
Thus, it has this chance of flexibility and self-correction. So,
for example, in Czechoslovakia in 1968 one of the basic
philosophical discussions dealt precisely with this problem of
freedom. Is freedom only recognized necessity? That's the
Hegelian concept. But the Czechs questioned this. Freedom
in the original Marxian sense, we asserted, is not just the
recognition of necessity. Freedom respects reality, but, at the
same time, it stresses that reality is not just a set of conditions as they are given. Epistemologically, this means that
there are no omniscient groups of people who can simply
define what reality is. Reality is a creative process for which
people are responsible. Certainly to move forward in history
and society humans must respect the given conditions; but
at the same time they never should declare those conditions
absolute. In Czechoslovakia in 1968 this intellectual temptation had to be checked. And this meant, of course, reopen-
ing the political problems involved, including the problem
of reevaluating the democratic heritage.[1]

In 1968 the name for the humanization of a socialist
society under such circumstances was democratization. By
this is meant that attitude of a mature socialist society which
takes itself and its creed really seriously, which understands
itself as really moving toward a classless society. This is a
society of citizens who are not antagonistic enemies of each
other, or of their own society as a whole, but who are united
in their common and fundamental social interests. And this
common social interest does not exclude diversities of outlook, of opinion, of culture, and of creed. These differences,

to be sure, are very real, and they create manifold tensions within society. We experienced this in Czechoslovakia in 1968. There were tensions in our society, new tensions, openly emerging and openly discussed. This was not without risks and dangers. And yet let me state clearly that in my opinion and in the opinion of the vast majority of the people in my country, these were very creative tensions. They did not cripple the progress of society, of *socialist* society. On the contrary, they enriched the community of which we were members. It was important, therefore, that these differences be tolerated and ventilated. Thus, in a mature socialist state, the citizen ceases to be its potential enemy. Every citizen receives his own fair share. And this is valid in all respects — politically, culturally, and ideologically.

An example of this from Czechoslovakia in 1968 can be cited. From my particular point of view as a theologian, Christian citizens got an amazingly new and full share in the public life of society. They were respected, not only as citizens but as *Christian* citizens. They were not just tolerated but encouraged to make their own distinctive contribution. Thus the monopoly of power and the monopoly of truth were checked. Christians tried to overcome these monopolies, and the communist party itself tried to overcome them in a remarkable and unexpectedly energetic move. Full support was given by all levels and segments of the population. In an open, democratic, socialist society a deeper unity of citizens was achieved, a unity realized in equality and freedom. This seems an important step forward on the path of humanization. We experienced the validity of the program which was once summed up by Rosa Luxembourg (a great representative of European democratic socialism and a Marxist thinker): "No democracy without socialism, but also no socialism without democracy." Our attempt here has been to see how these two traditions might be integrated.

What does this mean? Probably it means that within the context of a socialist society the best insights of the liberal and democratic tradition can be taken seriously and can be developed again. And here the third and concluding question must be asked: what about the third partner of the trinity, what about religion? Has religion anything to say, or to contribute to the quest for humanization?

THE RELIGIOUS PERSPECTIVE

In thinking of my own experience in Czechoslovakia in 1968, I do not hesitate to give a positive answer to this question. This is not just wishful thinking. This has been part of our fundamental living reality during these past few years. I refer to what was suggested earlier, the growing participation of religious people in the public life of society. The religious people (in our country, of course, predominantly Christians, because the Jewish population was liquidated by the Nazis) emerged not as outsiders of society but as insiders. The reasons for this lie deep, because the goal of democratic socialism in a sense corresponds, in our own conception, to the deepest insights of the biblical prophetic tradition. If we think of the vision of greater social justice as proclaimed by the Old Testament prophets, or again, if we think of the New Testament apostolic vision of the inalienable rights of every individual, then there is no doubt that the best insights of our own religious tradition point in the direction of a democratic socialism. So the involvement in the democratization of our society was for us not just a general trend into which we could be drawn from outside, but was very much our own necessary activity and task, and, in all modesty, our own contribution as well.

If the focus is narrowed to indicate in a few words the central and distinctive possible contribution of the religious tradition in this common goal of humanization, then one point especially which seems to be crucial should be emphasized. In my judgment, the basic contribution of the distinctively religious tradition toward the humanization of man's social life is an opening up of the perspective of hope. This is the classical religious perspective. It is well known that Immanuel Kant, when he tried to delineate the different areas of human life and culture, claimed quite justly that the basic sphere of religion is exactly this context of hope. *What can I hope for?* is the basic religious question of man. We know that today theology, both Roman Catholic and Protestant, seems to have learned from Kant. It emphasizes very strongly this basic perspective of hope.[2]

This new emphasis is justified, for this perspective of hope is truly unique to the biblical heritage. If there was something really new in the biblical contribution to mankind, it was certainly an opening up of history as a meaningful process, a breaking-through of all mythological or, as they are sometimes called, "ontocratic" structures. By this are meant those models of thought which consider the universe as closed, sacred, established in itself. Here everything is a perfect *kosmos*, everything is preordained, everything has its place and must be accepted basically as a divine order. This model of thought prevailed in both ancient mythology and philosophy. Biblical thought was utterly different. The basic biblical perspective is the perspective of Exodus. It proclaims the way out of captivity to preordained structures and established orders. It opens new possibilities for responsible human initiative in history.

Now if this is the basic vision of the biblical message (and in my opinion it clearly is), then this biblical vision has some important implications for the whole realm of politics. For there is one constant danger in the political sphere: the danger of fatalism. Politics is conceived as purely a game of power-politics, the El Dorado of the managers. The political structures are absolutized. Nationally, the "principalities and powers" of the establishment dominate the political scene. Internationally, the "big powers" divide their "spheres of influence" and declare them untouchable. Any threat to the "balance" — often arbitrarily defined — causes a power-political nemesis. The only responsible political attitude is "realism," that is, the cult of the given "law and order," of the status quo. Thus the sphere of politics is theoretically interpreted by many political scientists and politicians, while it is managed practically as the sphere of fate. In this atmosphere of "realism," responsible political quest and action are very much limited. The mood of "realism" is not far from the mood of fatalism.

It is exactly here that there might open a creative role for religion. But we must immediately qualify; certainly not for all religion. Much of traditional religion only cemented the spirit of fatalism. There is a religious tradition which is truly an "opiate of the people": an attempt to interpret the religious vision in purely transcendental and spiritual terms and to separate it from all secular implications in providing a purely "celestial" consolation. There is also a religious tradition sanctifying the status quo: an identification with the authority of God of what is powerfully present in the realm of political authority. And there is an outspoken religious fatalism: an understanding of God's Providence in terms of unchangeable destiny which must be accepted in an attitude of unquestioning resignation.

Thus there were always priests of fate, of the establishment, and of pious quietism. Yet there is also the biblical prophetic tradition, and this is very different. Certainly, the biblical vision of the Kingdom of God opens a dimension which is not simply "of this world." It transcends the potentialities of the world of man, of what can be achieved in history. It is the Kingdom of God. Yet this "transcending" kingdom is seen precisely in its dynamic relationship to men in history. The biblical God does not encourage any escapism. He is not an abstract transcendence, aloof from all secular concerns. On the contrary, he is the God involved in history, opening new possibilities, the God of the open future. He is all this in a concretely articulated way: his basic revelation in the Old Testament is the Exodus — an event of liberation. His basic revelation in the New Testament is the way of Jesus of Nazareth: his unconditional solidarity with men, particularly with those who are oppressed and poor. Thus, this is the way of his Kingdom, this is the way for man.

This vision opens new dimensions to human lives and action. It demythologizes the universe, which is no longer considered "sacred" and unchangeable, and it opens a perspective for meaningful commitment in history and society. This vision also opens a new perspective on man's understanding of himself. For biblical anthropology, man is neither a free angel nor a determined beast. Rather, the mystery of the human situation encompasses the knowledge that man has emerged from the earth. That means that he is limited, conditioned in all respects — psychologically, socially, culturally — while, at the same time, he knows that he is not just the sum total of those conditions. Man, created in the image of God, has a dimension of transcendence which is not simply to be identified with the horizon of man's social conditioning. From the biblical perspective, man is not just the sum total of human conditioning; rather, it is a part of his "condition of being human" to transcend his humanness as well, to have the limited possibility of steering and shaping his future, his destiny, by his action. Such action may be constructive or it may be destructive — the world depends on us as we depend on our world. In short, the biblical view of man as both mundane creature and as bearer of the image of God moves between two extremes: between an idealistic indeterminism (which claims that man is, so to say, just the free act, *actus purus*) and a materialistic determinism (which claims that man is simply the outcome of natural or social conditioning). Man in truth is neither an *actus purus* nor a determined product of nature and history. Man is, at one and the same time, conditioned, yet called to action and responsibility.

In the light of Exodus, in the light of God's involvement in the history of man in Jesus of Nazareth, the spell of fate is doubly broken. The world is demythologized. The "principalities and powers" do not have the ultimate keys of the world and of man. They are potent. The power-political element of the politician is to be taken very seriously. Moralism and idealism do not help. And yet, the politicians are not omnipotent. There is an open space and an open future for meaningful political work and action. So also, "reality" is not just what is given, the sum total of the determined conditions, the passive raw material for "the engineers of the future." Reality is also the challenge of the coming Kingdom of God, and man's response to that challenge in the search for greater freedom and justice.

To keep alive that spirit of challenge and to keep open that dimension of hope is a possible contribution of religious people to the world of politics today. Responsible politicians are not blind to that possibility. A word of John F. Kennedy to church leaders indicates this possibility: "Help me to create the climate in which bolder steps for a policy of peace and justice are possible again." Indeed, this "climate" is of ultimate importance if politics is to become and to remain a meaningful human activity. The dimension of sober hope is very much needed in all societies, perhaps particularly in both the United States and Czechoslovakia. The problems of these societies are overwhelming. Responsible citizens are often frustrated. Here a religious perspective of hope as a call to persevere in the effort toward humanization may make its modest contribution. It reminds us that the forces of chaos and oppression cannot eventually prevail. The world is not left irrevocably in the hands of political managers and manipulators. So it should not be left to them by us. Certainly the world of man is also the world of tanks. Yet the world of tanks is not the whole world of man. They must be challenged.

Every one of us is asked to get involved. In the perspective of hope this involvement is never in vain. It is worth while not to give up, but instead to strive, despite all possible and real difficulties, toward a change of all those conditions under which man is an oppressed, enslaved, destitute, and despised being.

NOTES

1. This point must not be misunderstood. Freedom is a much more difficult problem than any simple notion of democracy. So, for example, with respect to the American and Czechoslovakian situation, there is a strong tradition of so-called democratic freedom in American society and culture. That is, everyone is able to say anything he wants. Yet how often this possibility seems somehow unreal or irrelevant. Indeed, everybody says what he wants, but the key issue is whether man can achieve something or whether there are not tremendous blocks which effectively deny his "free" word and will. It is refreshing to be able to say everything, and the importance of this freedom should not be denied. To the contrary, it must be admired. But if one follows the political and social scene closely, how difficult it is to achieve a meaningful political and social change! Marxism has always been sensitive to and has criticized this ambiguity of the abstract conception of freedom. It has said that only after the socialist revolution — that is, after the elimination of the economic privileges and power of the minority which make ineffective "free speech," and so deny the most crucial element of its freedom — can democratic freedoms become concrete and effective. In short, I do not speak here in favor of a return toward an abstract liberalism, but for the maturation of a socialist society.

2. Some of the most creative Marxists today emphasize this same dimension of hope, and they emphasize it in opposing the interpretation of Marxism as historic fatalism. Why do Marxists like Ernst Bloch and others reexamine and bring to the foreground this element of hope? Because they want to revive the original Marxist tradition, claiming that history is not simply the development of certain predetermined ideas. It's an open process, for which we are responsible. So, for example, when the young Marx debated with Feuerbach, this was exactly the point at which he moved far beyond the heritage of both Hegel and Feuerbach. For Marx, materialism is not just a general theory about "matter" as the ontological starting point, but the emphasis on the creative possibilities of human action in history. In this sense the element of hope is extremely important for political action, for human action, and for the conception of freedom. Freedom is respect for the situation in which we are contextually involved and yet at the same time freedom involves the perspective of hope, a deep commitment to the search for new and broader possibilities of participation in society and for greater development of personality.

THE END OF THE ROAD AND A NEW BEGINNING
Richard Shaull

In thinking about the predicament of man in the modern world, one must experience today's world as one in which man is rapidly arriving at the end of the road, and can move ahead only as he makes a new beginning. The structures and institutions within which humans live seem to be bound by a given logic and process of development which make it impossible for them to respond creatively to the new challenges around them; consequently, only the negation of the old order and a qualitative change of structures will open the way to the creation of the new. Our predicament is due to the fact that, having arrived at this dead end, we are thus far unable either to bury the dead or to give birth to the new.

This is not a conclusion at which one willingly arrives. In fact, to admit it means to recognize the failure of all past efforts to renew and reform institutions and to move to the future with some sort of continuity with the given order. If I have reached this point, it is only that, in one sphere after another, I have been confronted by events which seem to offer no other option.

My first awareness of this came some years ago in Latin America when I was forced to discover that underdevelopment is not simply a stage prior to development, a situation caused primarily by the lack of certain essential resources and technology. Rather, underdevelopment is the product of a complex of economic, political, and social structures which together create a total social fact, a social order that makes development impossible. Under such circumstances, development depends upon *overcoming* that old order. It requires a break with the old, and the creation of a new framework of institutions in which new groups in society, working within a new political structure, can set new goals and move toward achieving them.

I was soon forced to a similar conclusion regarding relations between the United States and Latin America. Our patterns of economic and political domination are so strong and we are so tied to those groups determined to maintain the status quo there, that no mere increase in aid or improvement in communications will make a decisive difference. What is demanded is a fundamental change in policy. For this reason, the Alliance for Progress was destined to fail before it was launched; the emphasis it placed upon reform of structures in Latin America was not accompanied by any such basic change in the structures of our relationships.

Returning to the United States, I soon found myself facing the same sort of dead end in one place after another. The failure of our political institutions to meet the growing crisis in our large cities, together with the fiasco of the presidential elections of last year, provided evidence enough of the dead end to which we have come in that area. And as I have tried to examine more closely the way modern bureaucracy operates, I have become convinced that it possesses an inner logic of its own which is producing a society of the managers and the managed, and that the more efficiently it functions in solving small problems, the less capable it is of meeting new challenges in new ways. Confronted with the crisis in the university today, I see here one of the major examples of this dead end and of the tremendous price which we are forced to pay when we are incapable of moving to a new beginning.

But my most traumatic experiences of this phenomenon have occurred in the last few months. In one organization after another, I have found people completely immobilized because old forms of thought, old patterns of organization, and old structures seem completely inadequate; the only hope I see for moving beyond this point lies in the freedom to break out of that impasse and make a new beginning. This interpretation of the present moment will be so different from the experience and perspective of some people that it will make little sense; for others, it will represent a mistaken analysis of what is now happening and of the options before us. I have no way of proving I am right. If we are to act responsibly today, we must attempt to put together our experience of social reality, our careful analysis of it, and our tentative judgment about what is happening in the wider social and historical context. Only thus can we make a wager about how we can best move toward the future, or have a basis for responsible action. Any such conclusions will, of necessity, be tentative and will have to be submitted constantly to critical evaluation and tested out in practice. They will all be shaped by the conceptual tools we use and the perspectives within which we choose to operate.

In my own case, the terms for such reflection have been provided, to a large extent, by the historical experience of a particular community, and especially by one strand of historical understanding that has emerged and been operative in it. I refer to the Judeo-Christian tradition, and more specifically, to the eschatological and apocalyptic elements in it.

These elements have taken a variety of forms across the centuries, in thought as well as in radical communities. This perspective has been expressed in terms of a world view which makes very little sense to us today, but which may nevertheless provide some clues as to the nature of historical development and social change, even in the modern world.

At the core of this perspective, there is to be found, in biblical thought, a cluster of images that combine a variety of historical events and their interpretation, and that together provide a relatively coherent picture. The first of these is the Exodus story, which according to some Old Testament scholars, represents the central Old Testament paradigm. The decisive event in the formation of the Jewish people was their rebellion against slavery in Egypt, which led them to break away from a great civilization, move out into the desert, and make a new beginning. In later centuries, the prophetic perspective of God's messianic action in history constitutes a further development of this theme. Attempts to create a new order of justice and peace are often blocked by established structures; thus, according to Jeremiah, God must pluck up and break down, destroy and overthrow, in order to build and to plant.[1]

In both the Old and New Testaments, the mingling of apocalyptic imagery with the eschatological leads not only to a perspective on life and history that is radically oriented toward the future; it also focuses, at times, on the imminence of the end of the present order and the expectation of the irruption of a qualitatively new order. Perhaps most important of all is the central importance given in the New Testament, especially in Pauline thought, to the paradigm of death and resurrection. Out of this there emerges a perspective on life and the world in which life is seen as the fruit of death, the end is the occasion for a new beginning, and men are free to allow the old to die in trust that, out of that death, the new will emerge. It is quite true that this imagery, in the New Testament, often has no direct political implications. But when it functions in the wider context mentioned, it becomes a central element in the shaping of a broad historical perspective, in which the recognition of a dead end and the expectation of a new beginning become the central categories for understanding the world and working to change it.

Professor Marcuse has referred to the "radical heretical movements" that have arisen time and again in western Christian history. They have usually been marginalized and often severely persecuted by the institutional church, but their contribution has been recognized by many secular historians. Whatever the limitations of their outlook and witness, they have performed two tasks that have been important both in the life of the church and in the development of revolutionary social movements: (1) They have provided resources for a revolutionary perspective on social change; and (2) they have contributed to the formation of radical communities in which that perspective became operative in shaping life and action in society.

It is now clear that, in relation to the present social crisis, I am operating on the basis of two wagers rather than one: the first of these is that we can best understand and deal with our present situation when we view it in terms of a dead end and the occasion for a new beginning. The second is that the heritage that has provided much of the imagery and the concepts for such a perspective can be operative today and can contribute to the formation of communities, at the margin of the church's life, which will make some contribution to the struggle in which we are now engaged. This second wager demands a tremendous act of faith. If the history of the past hundred years is scrutinized, it is clear that the effort to humanize Christian beliefs (in order to negate the given social order and open the way for a new beginning) has been performed primarily by the great secular thinkers, not by Christian theologians. And the church, in many instances, has done everything possible to adjust

Christianity to the secular present and to provide a sacral validation for it. But given the impasse in which so many individuals and groups committed to working for radical social change now find themselves, even a discredited religious community and tradition has an occasion to prove itself. Whether or not such a wager is justified will be determined by our ability to respond to two challenges: the need for resources for constant social criticism, and the need for the formation of paradigmatic radical communities.

PRIORITIES IN SOCIAL CRITICISM

The test of the vitality of a religious community in the midst of a social struggle is its ability to equip its members for full participation in and commitment to that struggle at the same time that they maintain a critical attitude toward all that they think and do. Theoretically, theology should prepare us for that task, for it reminds us that our ultimate loyalty transcends every particular form of the immediate struggle, and provides us with resources for a constant process of radical iconoclasm. This is something much more easily said than done; the point has been made in almost all contemporary discussions of the question and need not be developed here.

But, in considering the relationship of religion to the contemporary encounter between Marxism and the liberal tradition, the point should be made that, whereas in the recent past the theologian has tended to focus his criticism on Marxism without challenging the basic presuppositions of liberalism, the time has now come when this situation should be reversed. If we are at a dead end in many of our structures and institutions and must discover how to embark upon a new beginning, then the theologian will find himself much closer to the Marxist than to the liberal, and will have to give primary attention, in his critical work, to exposing the limitations and failures of the liberal tradition.

We cannot and should not suddenly forget the horrors of the Stalinist era, the sclerosis of some socialist societies, or the dogmatism of many Marxist movements. But with all this, the fact remains that the Marxist who is faithful to his heritage functions in terms of dialectic and negation; he looks at and analyzes the given social order in light of its future transformation, and is motivated by a compelling drive to overcome the present order of things. What is demanded of him in the present situation is not a radical shift of perspective, but the demonstration of freedom to apply his own categories to social reality, to function in terms of his own method of social analysis without being bound by an outmoded and rigid metaphysic, and to analyze the new realities of our technological-bureaucratic society with the same rigor that Marx used in studying the structures of early capitalism—whatever the consequences of this might be for the revision of his own theory and *praxis*.

Concerning liberalism, the situation today is quite different. If it once represented a dynamic struggle for freedom, equality, and justice, a doctrine which demanded a high price of those who professed it, today these ideals have become slogans with little power to transform the world. And as it has lost its power to change society, it has placed increasing emphasis upon the defense of the only means it can accept for bringing about social change: gradual progress and reforms within the framework and according to the rules of the given social, economic, and political structures. To the degree that we are confronted by a situation demanding the creation of qualitatively new institutions and structures, this liberal dogma becomes the major obstacle to understanding and action.

Unable to perceive the dimensions of a dead-end situation, the liberal fails to grasp the new issues raised by radical social criticism; therefore, in discussing them, he can do no more than create a caricature of them. When, in his social analysis, he does probe deeper, he is unable to offer solutions

which match the radicality of his own analysis. Caught
within the limitations of his own perspective, he tends to dis-
miss as utopian speculation all attempts to create the qualitatively new; thus he excludes the one thing that could contribute to the creation of a new social order. Faced by a new
generation committed to the creation of a new future, the
liberal can only offer more and more of the same, or as Mario
Savio once put it, "the end of history."

What is even more serious is the fact that this liberal
dogma is maintained by a blatant distortion of western historical development. Confronted by those, in this country or
in the third world, who have lost hope in the present system
and are willing to risk violence and disruption in order to
overcome the old and create a new order, the liberal insists
that this is too costly and that the western nations — especially the United States — have been able to make decisive
progress by non-violent means toward the goals of liberty,
equality, and justice. As Barrington Moore has demonstrated
in his study, *The Social Origins of Dictatorship and Democracy*,[2] the real story is quite different. The stability, peace,
and progress toward our goals achieved in the nineteenth and
twentieth centuries have their foundation in three major
bloody revolutions which broke the power of the old order
and created conditions for a new beginning. The latest of the
revolutions performing this function was the American Civil
War. All people would, presumably, much prefer to achieve
goals by non-violent means. But what the liberal does not
recognize is that such a transition is possible only if those
now in power make room for the emergence of qualitatively
new solutions, and that it is precisely this which the liberal
ideology and strategy now make virtually impossible.

Radical communities within the church, dedicated to the
task of social criticism, will not have an easy time. But they
can help keep the debate going, and perhaps make some contribution to the exposure of the limitations of the liberal perspective, and free some people to move beyond it.

THE FORMATION OF PARADIGMATIC COMMUNITIES

In a revolutionary situation, the political task is primary, but that task is defined in a special way. It is a question of power to overcome the old order and to create a new order; for that reason the goal can never be the mere conquest of power within the old structures. Only the destruction of the old structure of power and its replacement by a new constitutes a revolution. This means that revolutionary politics is concerned simultaneously with two tasks: the exposure of the limitations and incoherence of the old order, and its eventual destruction; and the construction of the new from the ground up. And, as Marx clearly understood, this is ultimately the question of the creation of a new man.

Consequently, the revolutionary lives and works in a situation of constant tension. On the one hand, in the face of the suffering and injustice caused by the failure of the old order, he is driven by a tremendous sense of urgency; on the other hand, he must recognize that he is engaged in a long-term struggle, to be fought on many fronts against overwhelming odds. In his efforts to overcome the old as well as to create the new, he struggles against forces of the past which are also present in himself, as well as in his thought and action, and he is called upon to create that which has not yet been thought or formed. He finds himself under all the pressures of a guerilla unit in the heart of enemy territory; yet what is demanded of him is that he think clearly and critically, live and work experimentally, and concentrate his attention on the political task at hand at the same time that, as a person, he finds the resources to break free from his past and to live a new reality.

What this suggests is that the revolutionary will be free to participate creatively in the revolutionary struggle and to move toward the achievement of his goals only if he is able, in some way, to transcend it. That is something which does not easily happen. Some political movements may approximate it from time to time; some individuals will function in these terms; ultimately, however, such transcendence will come only as men and women participate in communities in which they are constantly forced to look at their political struggles in the light of broader historical and human perspectives, and in which their own lives are being transformed at the same time that they participate in the transformation of society. In other words, such communities help to make revolution possible because they facilitate the transition from a dead end to a new beginning in society, as they free persons and organizations to die and be resurrected again and again.

What are the prospects for the emergence of such communities in the midst of the revolutionary struggle today? One of the most encouraging developments in recent years, among those engaged in radical politics, is occurring at this point. It is here that radical religious movements can and should attempt to make a contribution. In fact, it is at this point that the relevance of such movements will be tested. For such movements are part of a tradition whose primary concern is the creation of a new man within a new order. The central symbols are related to this vision and task, and the historical experience of this tradition is the story of twenty centuries of success and failure in this area. Perhaps it is not too much to expect that this heritage should become operative once again in the present context, that it should contribute to the liberation of men and women from present forms of oppression, and provide models for new forms of social organization.

One example of this is provided by the Puritan movement in England at the end of the sixteenth century and during the early decades of the seventeenth centuries. In those communities, people who found themselves strangers in their own country gradually developed a way of life that was highly subversive, in the political as well as in the religious order. They worked out a new vision of reality, developed a new style of life and new forms of social organization, and found ways of surviving and functioning outside the religious establishment. As they gradually focused their attention more on the political than on the religious struggle, they developed what Michael Walzer has described as the first ideology, organization, and discipline of modern social revolution, and they played a decisive role in forming and supporting many of those who created the revolution of 1648.

Any attempt to do something like this today faces formidable obstacles, even among those small groups in the church that can be considered radical. One of the problems lies in the fact that, in the past, efforts to create a new man in a new social order have depended upon possession of a total world view and system of thought about man and society within which we could operate. Today, given the breakdown of the western philosophical tradition and the widespread theological crisis, we cannot hope to begin at this point. No old world view can be restored, or even translated into contemporary idiom. Nor can we expect to come up with a new world view; even if we could, it would not perform the function of ordering life which such total structures of thought once performed. However, it can be recognized that this loss also provides another option: to concentrate attention on the development of processes and the formation of communities by and in which men and women, in all the precariousness of their existence, can discover how to move from a dead end to a new beginning. When this event occurs, a new context will exist for serious reflection, and a broken-down memory will once again demonstrate its formative power.

Another problem is that of the relationship of such communities to the political struggle. The traditional pietistic influence is so strong in the Protestant religious community that even those groups which are most avant-garde fail to provide any tools for the integration of the personal and social aspects of life. On the other hand, those committed to political action tend to develop communities which represent radical political movements or new parallel social institutions. What is called for is that we break out of this false dichotomy and find ways by which those who are fully involved in a variety of political struggles can share in a common search for new ways of thought, new styles of life, and new structures of human relationships which will give them freedom to participate in a revolutionary struggle and perhaps provide them with new paradigms for social organization.

In the effort to develop such communities, there need be no concern to label them as religious or to limit them to those who consider themselves believers. In a secular world, the religious label makes little sense, so that the crisis of belief makes it impossible to draw such lines today. What is important is the freedom to work at the task of creating the new while carrying on a dialogue with a particular heritage and the experience of a historical community. For that to happen, those who participate in such an effort must be willing to wager that such an exploration is worth while, that it may provide clues for moving on into the future.

Those of us interested in the development of such radical communities are more concerned, at this moment, with creating them than with describing them. We are convinced that any discussion about them must be closely related to experience, and that thus far this experience is very limited. For the sake of a further exchange of experience, however, let me mention briefly a few conclusions to which some of us have come in the midst of various attempts, during the last year, to move ahead in this area. These conclusions represent both a report of progress and a series of unanswered questions. They are a report of progress because the groups to which we refer have succeeded in moving beyond a dead end, both in personal terms and in radical action, and are involved in creating something new. But a major question remains unanswered and takes various forms: will these groups be able to define the process they are now in and follow through

on it in such a way that their experience will have paradigmatic significance in a rapidly evolving social situation?

In comparing the experience of those groups that have
survived and moved ahead with those that have not, three
elements stand out as essentially important:

    1. *the awareness on the part of community members
of the precariousness of their own personal situation and
of the structural crisis of society, plus their insistence on
relating the two and finding some way of dealing with
both together;*

    2. *a willingness to engage in a process of self-
examination in the context of the wider social and cultural crisis, and to live with the results of such a process;*

    3. *a climate of trust which makes it possible for the
members of each group to be open to each other in this
process.*

These three things constitute the promise for the continued development of such communities; they also raise
questions which thus far have not been answered.

1. The members of one particular group began with a
rather keen sense both of their personal hang-ups and of the
oppressive nature of the present social system, and were convinced that these two were intimately related to each other.
They then began to explore the question, not by means of
abstract social analysis, but by asking themselves how the oppressive structures of society operated in their own lives,
within the family, the sphere of work and profession, life in
an urban society, and so on. In this way they came to see that
they, as well as other groups in the United States and abroad,
were victims of the present system, and that they were as
much a part of the revolutionary struggle as anyone else. As
they probed deeper into their own experience and did some
work on analysis of social systems, they not only arrived at a
clearer understanding of what the social struggle is all about,

but also moved ahead in terms of their own participation in it.

This has produced two rather surprising results. The first is the development of a more sharply defined self-identity over against the established order. This implies a stronger sense of alienation, a more positive interpretation of it, and a determination not to conform to the established rules of the game, but to explore and create new possibilities in various spheres of life. Second, a growing sense of the reality of oppression has been accompanied by a new experience of liberation. This has taken shape first of all within the life of the community itself, but has also been experienced, in a limited way, in other spheres of relationships. To the extent that this has happened, these communities and relationships create a certain environment of freedom within the wider context of social oppression. This in turn provides resources for sustained involvement in the struggle to create a new social order.

The unanswered question is whether people from a middle-class background, in a relatively stable and secure situation, will follow through on this process fast enough and probe deeply enough to be at the cutting edge of the revolutionary struggle. This is by no means certain. In fact, it is quite likely that a partial experience of liberation will blur one's awareness of the wider forces of social oppression and undermine the sense of urgency about confronting and overcoming the system as a whole.

If the process should continue, it will then raise other questions. As individual and corporate self-identity over against the system is strengthened, those who participate in this process will be more dissatisfied with their work in their professions and with the functioning of most of the institutions to which they are related. This will lead to conflict, to a sharper break with the established order, and to the search for more creative types of work and new forms of social organization. It will mean that the question of how to survive economically will be raised in an inescapable way; it will also mean a search for forms of community and strategies of action which will be really subversive, which will expose the basic contradictions within the system, deal with that system in a comprehensive way, and work for fundamental changes in it.

2. If we hope to be agents of social change today, it is not enough to discover that we are victims of oppression in an oppressive society and to participate in a political struggle to overcome the present oppressive structures. As Professor Manfred Halpern of Princeton University has recently pointed out, there is something historically unique about the quality of change in the modern age. "For the first time, man and all the political, social, economic, religious, intellectual, esthetic, and psychological systems by which he has so far organized his life, are persistently being rendered incoherent — elements are being destroyed; linkages between them, disconnected."[3] Consequently, revolution today is a question of creating "an enduring capacity to generate and absorb persistent transformation" which will express itself in social structures open to a constant process of change, capable of facing and overcoming persistent incoherence and of taking creative advantage of the opportunities which arise from the breaking of established connections. To be an authentic revolutionary today means to discover and live such a process in one's own life and be thus free to work for it in society as well.

This is something quite new, for which there are very few models. Most human experience thus far has been oriented toward security and stability, not toward a process of constant transformation in openness to the future. In fact, this orientation has been so dominant that even in the Christian community there has been little awareness of the radical break with it suggested by some of the most central biblical images and symbols.

In the eschatological perspective of the New Testament,

the institutions and structures of any given society belong to the old order that is passing away; they must be seen in the light of the new order that is already breaking in. Jesus Christ is not merely a historical personage who achieved perfect manhood at some point in the past; he is also the New Man, the goal toward which we are moving. And the doctrine of the Holy Spirit focuses on the constant and unexpected manifestations of power in the midst of life, capable of making all things new: the experience of life as growth in knowledge and creativity; the explosions of passion which upset the inertia of individual and corporate life; the experience of joy in the midst of suffering, of new meaning and depth in human relationships, and of new power for the mastery of the world and the forces in it.

For those who lived in the context of such events, even the experience of suffering and defeat was the occasion for the emergence of new possibilities; they could expect that, beyond the frustration of their best plans and the negation of their most cherished hopes, new and unexpected opportunities for meaning and fulfillment in life awaited them. Thus, they were free to let the order collapse and disappear when it was no longer viable, and could expect more adequate forms of social organization to emerge on the other side of change; they could also allow their own identity to be threatened ("dying daily" as Saint Paul put it) without being destroyed.

What is here suggested is that the New Testament does not provide a tight and systematic conceptual formulation of this, but describes the experience of a community of faith. And this, I believe, indicates where we should devote our energies. New images and symbols with power to shape life are likely to emerge only out of similar experiences on the part of people living in community. The vitality of such communities will depend upon their ability to give form to a process of constant transformation. And this in turn will depend upon the efforts of men and women who are committed to such a search and are willing to work at the development of a methodology for pursuing it.

If our experience of recent months is of any value, this process involves a constant critical examination of our values, goals, and life style in relation to the dynamics of our society; a discovery of the way by which people whose experiences and concerns are somewhat similar can encourage each other to persist in that process; and a willingness, on the part of each member, to allow his own self-identity to be called into question again and again. If this leads to a state of anxiety and crisis, it also opens the way for new images to emerge, and for people to organize their thought, their self-understanding, and their lives in new ways around new centers. Each achievement of this sort becomes not a final goal, or the basis for a new security, but rather the occasion for the repetition of this same process all over again. To the extent that this happens, a qualitatively new way of life takes shape, which should have revolutionary social implications. The Christian memory may still help to give us the courage for such a risky undertaking, for it affirms that, along this road, we will know and live the reality of creative forces constantly breaking old forms and creating new ones, and that precisely in this context we discover something of what the new humanity is all about.

3. If we are concerned with the formation of groups in which people not only have an increasing awareness of their situation of oppression as middle-class Americans, and of their need to create new social structures and a counter-culture, and also to participate in a dynamic process of persistent transformation through the constant negation of old values and the creation of new, then we can easily discern the overwhelming burden this places upon new forms of community life. In a situation of almost total precariousness, both of personal existence and social structures, the question raised is whether or not such communities can be, at one and the same time, *supportive* and *liberating*.

A variety of factors combine to create an unprecedented demand for supportive community, at the same time that they indicate something of the nature of the support required for revolutionary action today:

> In the face of the breakdown of all total world views and the failure of old dogmas to deal with a dynamic social reality, the revolutionary cannot seek security in any of these things. He must engage in constant social analysis, remaining open to new developments, seeking constantly to define and redefine his goals and strategy.

> Conditions of modern life contribute to the weakening of the former structures of personal existence, leading to a more fluid and unstable self-identity; at the same time, personal growth and responsibility in a rapidly changing world require that our selfhood be formed in an ongoing process of self-questioning, death, and resurrection.

> The new sensibility of youth combined with the failure of reason to deal with these dimensions of experience and with social reality have produced a situation in which the tendency is to act on the basis of anger, frustration, and rebellion. But unless such feelings are tempered by a new rationality, they can lead many of the more sensitive of a new generation to self-destruction and to action that is politically ineffective.

> The apparently overwhelming power of the established order, the internalized burden of our past which we all carry with us, and the frustrations produced by the inner logic of sclerotic institutions, all work together to shatter our hopes for a new order. This situation can be overcome only through the miracle of a community of shared hope.

> The increasing polarization in our society and the necessity for the creation of a counter-culture and counter-institutions, may well mean that a long-term revolutionary struggle can be carried on only as men and women,

throughout the social fabric, discover how to survive economically at the margin of or outside the system. This is possible, in any significant way, only as a collective effort.

Under these circumstances, it is not surprising that there is an interest in and drive toward community that was not so evident in radical circles even a few decades ago. In some instances, the new communes and other such ventures have met a felt need; in others, they have led to much frustration. Common living and the talking through of personal problems does not automatically prove liberating, and any experience of community that does not offer a new experience of freedom can contribute very little to the present revolutionary struggle. Such freedom, in the present situation, must take certain specific forms:

It will be freedom to live without the security of closed systems of thought; freedom to seek understanding in constant critical interaction with others in the midst of radical political action; freedom to challenge every tendency — in oneself and in others — and to absolutize one's own perspective and ideology.

Likewise, in the realm of personal relationships, freedom means finding support from others without depending upon them, without the exclusiveness of closed groups. In fact, that community relationship will be most successful and valuable that makes people less and less dependent upon it.

Community in which people burden each other with their own problems can produce only a vicious circle of increasing frustration. The experience of freedom comes from the sort of sharing of life in which people are freed from the burdens of their past and dare to make a new beginning, to perceive options they were formerly unaware of, and to find a type of interaction with each other in which each is challenged to be more creative.

Freedom is a matter of each person moving beyond where he happens to be, according to his own process, with its own unique rhythm. A liberating community is one that facilitates this process for each of its members; it creates a framework for a group process which supports rather than violates the authentic development of its members.

THE CHRISTIAN STORY IN RADICAL PERSPECTIVE

It is still too early to say much about the specific form which such communities will take. The answer to that question will come primarily from the experience of groups engaged in such efforts; it will be aided more by critical discussion of such experience by those in many diverse situations than by any theoretical prescriptions. One question, however, can be raised: does it make any sense for those who are still related in some precarious way to a historical community of faith to work on this problem from the vantage point of their particular heritage? Some of us are willing to make this wager, because we believe that in the Judeo-Christian tradition and experience may be discovered some elements for creative struggle with this issue as it has just been raised.

The New Testament story is the description of man's freedom for self-giving love. Jesus of Nazareth, in whom that love is realized, is not an isolated individual who has achieved the impossible against the hostile forces of man and the universe. He is the incarnation of that love which is the ultimate reality of the cosmos as well as of the historical existence of man. The christological formulations affirm that the appearance of such love in human form is not merely his (or our) achievement; it is something that happens to him, and to us. By declaring and demonstrating that Jesus has power over demons, the New Testament writers affirm that love operates in a world in which the power of all those mythological and historical forces that enslave and threaten to destroy man has been broken. Likewise, the eschatological language about Jesus expresses the conviction that the *agape* which he incarnated is the power of the future, and will be operative in a world moving toward a new order.

The New Testament Christology has implications for the realm of personal existence as well. Justification by faith means that we need not attempt to establish our own worth or to justify our actions. We can begin by accepting the fact that our worth has been established and that we have been accepted; consequently we are free to be honest with ourselves in relation to others. Moreover, the most elemental experience of the early Christians, described as the work of the Holy Spirit, was that of a power which overcame their pasts and set them on a new road, released hidden energies within them, and led to new depth of personal experience and of interpersonal relationships.

What we have here, in this imagery, is a perspective on life and the world in which men are free to run the risk of trust, and to give themselves to others without making claims upon them. Self-giving is not seen primarily as sacrifice, self-denial, exposure to the threat of others, but as the road that leads to an ever richer life of personal fulfillment and to the creation of a new world. We could say that it provides the context for the development of Eros, a great love destined to overcome the old order of personal and social existence, to break its bonds and create the new.

Obviously, this story as it has come down to us no longer has the power to create or sustain this perspective on life and the world. But that need not prevent accepting such a perspective or putting it to the test. For it is just possible that, in communities of men and women involved on the cutting edge of the revolutionary struggle, for whom this Christian memory is in some way still operative, new images and symbols may emerge which will once again contribute something to the shaping of life and thought.

NOTES

1. Jer. 1:10.

2. Barrington Moore, *The Social Origins of Dictatorship and Democracy* (Boston: Beacon Press, 1966).

3. Manfred Halpern, "A Redefinition of the Revolutionary Situation" (unpublished paper).

CHRISTIAN RESPONSIBILITY IN A TIME THAT CALLS FOR REVOLUTIONARY CHANGE
John C. Bennett

In the lifetimes of many of us in the United States there have been at least three quite different ways of thinking and feeling about the relationship of Christianity to the radical transformation of society. There was the liberal progressivism of the Social Gospel, a form of Christianity which had all the openness to the future that now dominates theologies of hope and theologies for revolution. There was, next, a stage of Christian thinking that began with disillusionment over the assumption of the almost inevitable progress often attributed to the Social Gospel and that projected both an inhibiting "realism" about what is possible in history, and as well, a view of the Gospel that in varying degrees shifted attention away from the problems involved in political and social change to a theological preoccupation with the revealing and redeeming acts of God in past history.

Generalizations of this kind are a caricature of the thought of many individuals who might be classified as representatives of "neo-orthodoxy" or "Christian realism." The struggle against National Socialism, including political support of World War II, came during that second period. For the most part the "social action" of that period was action against institutional embodiments of evil so demonic that victory over them was the chief object of hope. In order to achieve victory over National Socialism, Christian ethics usually sanctioned the second world war, and in order to prevent the extension of Stalinism, Christian ethics often accepted the political and military strategies of the cold war, including the whole apparatus of nuclear deterrence with its terrifying moral dilemmas. The shadow of nuclear war, of the possible annihilation of large populations, of the destruction of civilized life, was always present; thus the hope of preventing such a catastrophe overshadowed more positive hopes for a transformed society.

BEYOND CHRISTIAN REALISM: THE STRUGGLE FOR A NEW HOPE

Today we are in a new stage. The forward-looking social activism of the Social Gospel is with us again, but in a much more radical form. It is no longer guided by what now seem bland expectations of easy progress. It is in revolt against world poverty. It is moved by the desperate need of revolutionary change by whatever means may seem necessary in the third world. It is in rebellion against the American imperialism that seems bent on preventing revolution in the third world. The war in Vietnam has become the symbol of cruel and mindless use of military power and of a counterrevolutionary foreign policy. These views of the American position in the world are widely held in the United States, both inside and outside the churches. They are very common among the present generation of students and also among their teachers. The nation as a whole, while not accepting the moral criticisms of American policy, has begun to recognize the failure of the American attempt to impose an American solution on Vietnam. President Nixon has begun to make many inconsistent sounds about a new foreign policy.

There are important connections between the revolutionary impulses in the third world and the new revolutionary black consciousness in the United States. The revolt against the effects of white racism and against the remarkable failure of the American economy to solve the problems of urban poverty provides, even in the midst of American affluence, some understanding of the nations where poverty is the dominant condition.

The Christian ethic of this third stage is not content with negative victories over evil. It sees no easy or gradual ascent ahead to a world society of justice and peace, but it does project a hope for such a society. There may be some utopian illusions in the hope, but there are few such illusions about the road to these goals. Bitter struggles, discontinuities, revolutions involving violence are expected in many situations. Something more than a pragmatic movement in this country from one form of a mixed economy to another is sought. The powers that now control the private sector of the American economy have too much responsibility for the remaining poverty, for the pollution of the environment, and for the dominance of the military to escape a basic revolt against their control. Hope for a new economy that is responsive to social needs and yet will avoid the cultural totalitarianism and the inhuman bureaucratization that have bedeviled most of the contemporary "socialistic" experiments has become a positive force. Those whom it inspires will not accept the vetoes or the inhibitions of a Christian realism hardened in the early 1950s. Not only those who represent the "theology of hope" but a whole new generation of Christian activists insist on breaking through many of the stereotyped limits of the possible that were dictated by an earlier theology.

Some of the theological vetoes and inhibitions referred to were formed around the politics of the cold war. During the period of Stalinism, and while there seemed to be unity in international Communism, the churches and theologians in the non-Communist world thought in terms of an un-changing ideological, political, and military struggle between the two blocs for control of the world. The official atheistic dogma and anti-religious policies in Communist countries and Communist parties often turned this conflict into a holy war. The ecumenical movement centered in the World Coun-cil of Churches always preserved a precarious transcendence of this conflict between the nations, partly because of a theological stance that remained critical of the pretensions of the "free world" and partly because there were member churches in Communist countries of eastern Europe. The holy war psychology remained dominant in the Roman Cath-olic Church until the Vatican Council; this was especially true in the United States, where Roman Catholicism was more dominated by the spirit of an absolutistic anti-Com-munism than was the theological and ecclesiastical leader-ship of ecumenical Protestantism. However, there were no greater zealots of the holy war against Communism than the conservative Protestants who edited the journal *Christianity Today*, and the members of other Protestant movements further to the right.

Changes in the Communist world familiar now to all readers of these pages have prepared the way for the aban-donment of the hostility and the politics of the cold war, but the older generation in religion and politics has had difficulty responding to this new situation. The rhetoric of the politicians and the generals most responsible for the war in Vietnam reflected the views that had been dominant in the early 1950s. Very slowly changes have come on official levels; on the whole, religious leadership and the academic community were ahead of the politicians and the general public. Fortunately, generations change on both sides of the ideological conflict. Today the student generation in the United States that never knew Stalinism is ready to make a fresh start in the relations between the United States and the Communist nations. It is not at all tempted by the dullness or the oppressiveness of Communist bureaucracies, but it is repelled by what remains of the old anti-Communist belligerence of which the war in Vietnam is the horrible fruit, and it has no illusions about the moral claims of American democracy as the way of life at home or as a political and military power abroad.

I welcome these new horizons and have, for more than a decade, consistently opposed theological and political thinking dominated by the cold war or by the more negative dogmas of Christian realism. At the same time, two warnings should be offered. One is that the understanding of the sin and finiteness of man taught by Reinhold Niebuhr in his criticism of liberal progressivism should not be forgotten. Niebuhr's thought was based upon a broad empiricism rather than on theological dogmatism, though he found important clues in the biblical and theological tradition. The other warning is that the theologians of revolutionary hope should not be permitted to mislead us into assuming that there is any sure movement from a redemptive eschatology or messianism to secular utopias, or even to secure secular structures of justice and peace. There is hope that humanity can learn from the massive evils in which it is involved and from the presence of new technical possibilities of a better life for all. After recognizing sin in the form of pride, greed, and the will to power that have always appeared on every level of human advance to corrupt it beyond the expectation of previous prophets of hope, and after learning from our experience of the tendency of human collectives to be so easily persuaded of their own righteousness and so limited in their discernment of the virtues, the needs, or the natural fears of those who are on the other side of a conflict, it is still possible to avoid particular a *priori* limits to the solutions of problems.

If the realists of an earlier period, in their rejection of the illusory hopes of their predecessors, found correctives for those illusions in one aspect of Christian teaching, we may now find correctives for the complacent acceptance of limits to what is possible. The theology of hope may go too far in deducing or appearing to deduce hopes for political revolutions from the resurrection or from the invasion of the coming Kingdom of God into our history, but they have given back to us a sense of an open future. They have helped to remove the theological damper from the struggles of the hungry and the poor, of those who are humiliated and deprived because of their race, of those who seek the conditions of peace.

There are three sources of hope which may, through their interaction, make possible what all of us are now calling a more human existence for the human race. The first is the image of God in man. This image is universal, an essential aspect of man's created being which is often hidden or distorted by all that the theologians have said about sin but which is never, as some theologians have suggested, a lost image. The second is the redemptive work of God within his creation, the God of the past and the present as well as of the future. Christians see the evidence of this redemptive work in the events, the persons, and the movements associated with the coming Jesus Christ. They should not claim that it can be seen from no other vantage point, but they can truly say that what they have known in Christ is for them the criterion by which other signs of the grace of God in the world can be recognized. But this should be said in a spirit of openness to new and different signs of the redemptive and gracious working of God, not in the spirit of those who possess a monopoly of truth or salvation, as has too often been the case within the Church. The third source of hope is the learning from massive events that show conclusively the ways of death and the ways of life for man.

Neither the given fruits of the image of God nor any human goodness that is a gift of particular Christian mediations of grace can take the place of these new lessons from history. Professor Raines shows very effectively that changes within Christian understanding come from the effect of changes in the world upon the mind of the Church. Our era is a time of rapid change, a time in which men have recently seen such horrors as Auschwitz, as well as Hiroshima and other cities that have been wiped out by weapons of mass destruction. It is a time when men live under the shadow of missiles pointed at the cities of both the United States and the Soviet Union. It is a time when they know that half or more of humanity is entering into dynamic history free for the first time from the old colonial domination, yet still hungry, still in need of radically new structures of political and economic life, and threatened by new forms of colonial power from both east and west. So men know that they cannot longer live by old assurances or old vetoes. They must move into the future with the hope of choosing the way of life. If not, then they drift by default into the way of death.

Little optimism would be possible if this move were based on any one of these sources of hope alone. It is the interaction among them that may make the difference. From this viewpoint, it is possible for those who work primarily in the light of any one of the sources of hope to find their vocations, but there would be great gain if, in doing so, men would raise their eyes to see the contribution of those who have chosen other vocations based upon other sources of hope. Interaction does not depend on conscious cooperation or collaboration; tension, as well as such cooperation or collaboration, can be expected. Yet, such conscious cooperation or collaboration should be possible on an increasing scale between those who see current problems from a Christian

perspective and those who see them from a Marxist perspective. It will become possible when Christians abandon those
aspects of their tradition that have made religion an opiate
for the feelings of the weak and the consciences of the
strong, and when Marxists learn from Stalinism and other
forms of post-revolutionary excesses to find their own way
to freedom and to the sources of meaning that political and
economic changes alone do not provide.

Let us deal briefly with some of the issues raised for
Christians by Marxism because these issues confront us when-
ever situations require revolutionary change.

THE NEW MARXIST-CHRISTIAN DIALOGUE

Whatever we may think about the relevance of Marxist
analyses of history and of social forces for a particular country, Marxism has provided in most countries both the frame
of thought and the faith for living to those who seek revolutionary change. Today the conflict between tired Marxist
orthodoxies too long the official doctrine of political establishments and various forms of "revisionism" complicate the
picture extremely. The conflict between atheistic Marxism
and Christianity has often taken the form of a holy war. The
atheistic or anti-religious dogmatism of all forms of Marxism
until the beginnings of the current Christian-Marxist dialogue
has been a great misfortune, despite the fact that there was
much justification for it in view of the actual performance
of the churches. Long before the current dialogue there was
an effort by many Christians to preserve a real openness toward Marxism, to combine rejection of particular historical
embodiments of Marxism with a recognition that Marxism
has been the bearer of a true revolutionary imperative, that
it has filled a vacuum left by the default of Christians, that its
anti-religious stance is a judgment upon the churches. There
was a good deal of what one might call pre-revolutionary
dialogue between Marxists and radical Christians and there

have been interesting experiments with a Christian Marxism or a Marxist Christianity. Quite apart from these, openness to Marxism as the bearer of much truth, and the freedom of many Christians from self-righteous condemnation of Marxist atheism should be remembered. These combined with a strong self-criticism by the churches for their failure to bear any adequate message to the victims of early capitalism.

The following passages are illustrations of this outlook. Both are from the year 1948. The first is from the report of one of the sections of the Amsterdam Assembly of the World Council of Churches.

> *Christians should ask why communism in its modern totalitarian form makes so strong an appeal to great masses of people in many parts of the world. They should recognize the hand of God in the revolt of multitudes against injustice that gives communism much of its strength. They should seek to recapture for the Church the original Christian solidarity with the world's distressed people, not to curb their aspirations towards justice, but, on the contrary, to go beyond them and direct them towards the only road that does not lead to a blank wall, obedience to God's will and His justice. Christians should realize that for many, especially for many young men and women, communism seems to stand for a vision of human equality and universal brotherhood for which they were prepared by Christian influences. Christians who are beneficiaries of capitalism should try to see the world as it appears to many who know themselves excluded from its privileges and who see in communism a means of deliverance from poverty and insecurity.*[1]

There follow strong criticisms of Marxist Communism as it was embodied in particular nations and parties, especially of its promise of complete redemption of man in history, its ruthless dealing with opponents, its claim upon the whole person, and its attempts to establish control over every aspect of life. However, these criticisms would now be admitted by many contemporary Marxists. The Amsterdam criticisms of actual tendencies within capitalism and their human effects were also very strong.

The other passage is from a statement of the bishops of the world-wide Anglican communion at their 1948 conference in Lambeth.

> *We have to admit that the Christian Church through the formative decades of the industrial era showed little insight into what was befalling human society. It was still thinking in terms of feudalism. The Church of England was identified almost completely with the ruling classes, as were the churches of central and eastern Europe. Its own economy had the marks of a dying feudalism or latterly of bourgeois society. Apart from provision for education of the poor and the work of some churchmen for the emancipation of slaves and of children in the factories, it was slow to take the initiative in the desperate fight for social justice. A churchman here or there, a Christian group here or there wholeheartedly upheld the cause of the oppressed, but only in more recent times has the church begun to make a radical critique of Western society, and to provide a climate that is not hostile to revolutionary spirits.*[2]

This is a very frank confession by a conference of bishops of the failure of the churches. It would be difficult for those who hold this view to take self-righteous attitudes toward the anti-religious outlook of Marxism. Both these statements reflect an entirely different spirit from that which has inspired Christian anti-Communist crusades and foreign policies influenced by the psychology of the "holy war."[3]

During the 1950s churchmen in the western nations, even when they tried to preserve self-criticism and openness toward Marxists, were horrified by Stalinist terror in the Soviet Union and in eastern Europe, so that they generally supported western governments in their efforts to contain Communist military power.

Today there is a new situation in the relationship between Christians and Marxists. Diversity among Communist countries has freed Marxism as a way of thinking from control by any single political establishment. Marxists in many countries have rejected not only Stalinism in its Soviet form but, more broadly, the dehumanizing and oppressive forms of control by both governments and party leaders. The fact that this form of humanistic Marxism developed within the Czech Communist party is significant, even though for the time being it may have been effectively suppressed by Soviet power. There are similar currents in Yugoslavia, where more freedom is enjoyed, and in the Marxist parties of western Europe.

Professor Marcuse has stated: "There is something in the basic Marxian conception itself which seems to continue repressive tendencies and extend them from the old societies to the new. And I believe that the present rebellion of the militant youth is largely directed against this ambiguity in the Marxian conception and strategy themselves. Or, in other words, this rebellion invokes tendencies in Marx which seem to have been repressed by Marx himself. This rebellion invokes forgotten liberating and libertarian forces in Marxian theory itself."

This Marxist self-criticism at a deeper level than self-criticism of particular policies and actions is one of the essential new factors.

Another new factor is the development both of strong Christian self-criticism and a Christian commitment to social revolution in many situations. The most dramatic change has taken place in Roman Catholicism, which was so strongly anti-Marxist in its teaching. Even at the top level, the Roman Church is encouraging dialogue with Marxists. This has opened doors that were tightly shut a decade ago. And there is also a new revolutionary spirit, especially among younger priests and laymen, both in western Europe and in the third world. Catholic radicalism in Latin America, supported by courageous bishops in a few countries such as Brazil and Chile, is one of the most promising developments in the Christian world. It has been as unexpected as it is promising.

The new dialogue between Christians and Marxists which either accompanies political collaboration or prepares the way for it has produced in a few situations at least a sense of mutual need. Professor Jürgen Moltmann has described the remarkable changes among Marxists who hope to receive from Christians the dimension of transcendence lacking in Marxism, as well as help in the search for the meaning of life that cannot be assured by a successful political and economic revolution. It is ironic that some Marxists have shown disappointment that Christian theologians, in their concern for immediate relevance to the problems of society, have often avoided emphasis on the transcendence of God. Moltmann quotes a fascinating passage from Professor Milan Prucha, a Marxist scholar in Prague: "Our Christian friends have awakened in us the courage for transcendence. For a long time we Marxists have tried to criticize and retard the Christian striving for transcendence. Should it not, rather, be our task to encourage the Christians to be more radical in their striving for transcendence?"[4]

Professor Marcuse's recognition that Marxism in itself needs correction if a false political absolutism is to be avoided, and the search of some Marxists for a meaning in life beyond the political to which Christian theologians are expected to witness, indicate that Marxism is not necessarily conceived by Marxists as a self-sufficient doctrine. Christians may admit to the same attitude concerning their faith and their theology. They may hold a variety of views about the extent to which Christian thinking can find its own correctives in biblical sources if Christians are delivered from the blinders preventing them from discerning those correctives. Whatever they think about the theoretical adequacy of Christian truth for all situations may be theologically interesting but in practice it is not very relevant, since the churches and Christian theologians regularly need to be delivered from such blinders by ideas and perceptions independent of distinctively Christian sources.

The mere fact that such people are now pressed by people in the third world and by blacks in the United States who demand movement now toward a new society has often changed their priorities as Christians. What happened in a limited way as a result of the revolt of the industrial workers against early capitalism is happening again. Now as then the language of the revolt is often Marxist. Indeed we can say that without this Marxist challenge Christians have not grasped their responsibility as Christians. It is the mutual need that Christians and Marxists have for each other that makes the current dialogue new and important. In the United States, where it is difficult to find a Marxist for dialogue, Christians will be influenced by the effects of the dialogue elsewhere. It may be that this influence will come chiefly on a rather rarefied theological level, as it comes from Europe, but the dialogue and the collaboration between Christians and Marxists in the third world and especially in Latin America may have a transforming effect on the Christian understanding of the United States' role in the world. It remains to be seen how much the black revolution in this country, and the response of white Christians and the dominant churches to it, will be influenced by a reconsideration of the relationship between Christianity and Marxism.

THE END OF AN ERA: THE QUESTION OF REVOLUTION

This volume is a response to the widespread conviction expressed in the title of Professor Schaull's essay, "the end of the road and a new beginning." There is nothing new about the proclamation of social hope, of an open future which will give meaning to present strivings. This has usually been seen in the United States in terms of constitutional changes, orderly progress, gradual reform. In the 1930s there was a brief flurry of revolutionary talk, for the depression seemed to be the end of a road, and Marxist interpretation of historical forces influenced American radical thought. Reinhold Niebuhr's *Moral Man and Immoral Society* was the great Christian book on social and political philosophy and ethics of that period; while not Marxist in its ultimate doctrines, it was largely Marxist in its view of history. Indeed Niebuhr wrote it when he was in the process of abandoning a pacifist form of social ethics, but his chief concern was not the need of military force in international relations but the real possibility that violence might be necessary in the domestic struggle for justice. Niebuhr believed that any social changes brought about through the ballot would be threatened by the dominant economic groups and that violence might become unavoidable in the resistance to counterrevolutionary forces. The sense of crisis, of the possibility of social advance through catastrophe, was very much in the minds of radical Christian thinkers at that time. The lesson of European forms of fascism was not lost on Americans. Only a few years later American Christians were almost united in their support of a war that was viewed as a war against fascism, especially in its National Socialist form. In principle, the use of violence was accepted as justified by the most influential Christian thinkers, including Reinhold Niebuhr, Paul Tillich, Karl Barth, and Archbishop William Temple, and by most denominational and ecumenical councils.

The war itself ended the interest in revolutionary possibilities in this country. The New Deal plus the war economy seemed to provide what "new beginning" was necessary, and the disillusion caused by Stalinism, in spite of our wartime alliance with the Soviet Union, ended the attraction of Marxism. Even Christian Socialism in its non-Marxist forms gave way to the postwar acceptance of the mixed economy with its euphoric affluence. I was involved in the attempt to create a moderately leftist Christian movement called "Christian Action." This initially had considerable support because it inherited the results of a previous movement once known as "The Fellowship of Socialist Christians," and later as "The Frontier Fellowship." It took over that movement's journal, *Christianity and Society*, edited by Reinhold Niebuhr. But Christian Action petered out because there seemed to be no unifying cause, or, as Liston Pope once put it, there was a difficulty in organizing a parade for a mixed economy. There was no talk of revolution; Marxism was regarded as an irrelevance.

The scene has changed completely. We see at least the following elements in this change: the radical black consciousness; the discovery that the period of euphoric affluence had been accompanied by the decay of the cities and continuing poverty — both urban and rural — affecting the lives of from thirty to forty million people; the impact of the revolutionary consciousness in the third world, which became related to the American black revolution; and the revolt of students, sometimes against the meaninglessness of their middle-class affluence, sometimes against the seeming irrelevance of their education, and always against the Vietnam war, as both a threat to them and as a moral outrage.

Professor Shaull's essay brings into focus two of the new factors mentioned: the need for revolutionary change in the third world, especially in Latin America; and the sense that only a change of similar proportions in this country can remove it as a counterrevolutionary force from the backs of the third-world countries. Vietnam seemed to prove this second point. For a decade Professor Shaull has been the chief American theologian concentrating on these issues. Each new statement by him relates more clearly and forcefully "the end of the road" in the third world to "the end of the road" in the United States.

There has been a considerable discussion of these issues of revolution in world-wide Christian circles. The Geneva

Conference on Church and Society in 1966 was the most influential event in the movement of thought within the churches on the subject of revolution. Professor Paul Ramsey, whose thought stands out in sharp contrast to the emphases in this volume, has given me partial credit (though in the form of a gentle accusation) for the revolutionary emphasis at Geneva, because, as editor of one of the preparatory volumes, *Christian Social Ethics in a Changing World*, I used an essay by Professor Shaull as the first chapter. I doubt if that editorial decision made so much difference. The Geneva Conference from beginning to end rocked with the subject of political and social revolution. Indeed its official theme was "Christians in the technical and social revolutions of our time." The technical revolutions with their transforming effects on culture which were not a matter of political choice were taken for granted. But much emphasized also were the deliberate political actions designed to change the location of power or the possessors of power, and to expedite the processes of modernization. It was usually strong and radical voices from Latin America that kept this form of revolution before the conference. Often it was said that the Colombian Father Camillo Torres, who died as a guerilla priest, was the great hero and martyr of the conference.

The Geneva Conference was of enormous importance in getting the discussion of these issues out in the open and on the agenda of the churches. Most of the more radical statements about revolution came in speeches and in informal discussions. The more carefully prepared reports were quite cautious in dealing with unconstitutional or violent forms of social change. Most of the official speaking was about economic development rather than about revolution in the third world. Geneva did pose the revolutionary question, however, with honesty and a sense of urgency.

There is one generalization that can be made as a result of the discussion in the Geneva Conference and in subsequent ecumenical meetings: theological permission for engaging in revolutionary activities could now be assumed. Ethical inhibitions, sometimes inspired by pacifism, still remained in some circles and, when not made absolute, these should remain so far as the use of violence is concerned. Also, contextual questions concerning the need of political revolution, the possibility of successful revolution, and the particular ways in which even an externally successful revolution may be corrupted, remain and will always remain. A major weakness of all this current discussion of revolution is that it seldom comes down to cases, to a consideration of what the resources for revolution are in a particular situation and what the nonrevolutionary or counterrevolutionary forces will be doing. The Marxists have emphasized the importance of social readiness for revolution in particular historical situations. Much can be learned from this note of realism in their thought. In this connection there is also a difference between western Europeans and churchmen in the third world, not only because the former come from countries which have reasonably successful social and political systems, but also because they remember so well the National Socialist revolution. That had many of the external marks of a revolution, yet it was demonic. Many Christians were deceived by it. Because of this, Professor Roger Shinn raised at Geneva the question of the criteria for distinguishing among revolutionary movements.

However, it was the revolutionary action against the National Socialist state in the Church struggle in Germany that may have done more than anything to remove the theological veto on resistance to political authority which still had some force, especially in Lutheranism. The National Socialist revolution was a warning against false revolutions; but the fact that Christians brought up on the authority of the injunction in Rome XIII against disobedience to political authorities found themselves ready to engage in conspiracy and tyrannicide against the National Socialist regime is part of the background of the current theological discussion of the possible justification of revolutionary activity.

The most careful discussion of the theological and ethical aspects of revolution took place at a conference in Zagorsk, near Moscow, in the spring of 1968. (While this discussion was carried on in one of the countries that fears revolution most, Russians outside the conference were not influenced by it!) This conference was called jointly by the Church and Society department and the Faith and Order Commission of the World Council of Churches and was attended by about thirty-five persons from all parts of the world. There were eight Roman Catholic participants who played an important part in all the discussions. One of the sections of the conference report dealt with the problem of revolution. Here the ambiguity in the use of the word "revolution" was noted, and especially the confusion between unplanned revolutionary cultural changes and revolution as "the changing of the social class holding economic and political power, mainly the transformation of the system of property, with a consequent replacing of political leaders." Concerning revolution in the latter sense, the conference stated:

> Christians in the revolutionary situation have to do all in their power to exercise the ministry of reconciliation to enable the revolutionary change to take place non-violently or, if this is not possible, with the minimum of violence. But we must realize that some Christians find themselves in situations where they must, in all responsibility, participate fully in revolution with its inevitable violence.
>
> Christian theology warns us against sacralizing either the status quo or the revolution. This warning is all the more necessary since the revolution is menaced most by the self-justification which it produces and which it gives to men when it yields to the temptations of false messianism and the fury of self-righteousness.
>
> Common membership in an inclusive church should remind us of the full humanity of the political adversary or enemy.[5]

An exegesis of those few sentences would provide most of the generalized Christian teaching available about revolution. They contain the permission to participate in revolutionary violence, always the most controversial point. What was said at Zagorsk had been cautiously suggested at Geneva in 1966 in the official reports but, for all the general talk about political revolution at Geneva, the question of revolutionary violence was barely touched upon in its reports. At Geneva and in 1968 at Uppsala the emphasis was on "development" rather than on "revolution." However, there were always those present who emphasized that present international aid to development tends to strengthen the ruling oligarchies in some countries and to provide little real economic change for the people. In the report of the section of the Uppsala Assembly on world economic and social development there is a cautious paragraph, obviously full of compromises in the drafting, that permits participation in revolutionary violence; but it is clearly stated that "revolution is not to be identified with violence."[6]

One of the issues that complicates the discussions of revolution by the official Roman Catholic and Protestant bodies (now united in a joint committee of the World Council of Churches and the Vatican on Society, Development and Peace) is the even greater hesitancy of the Vatican to sanction revolutionary violence. There is a passage in Pope Paul's encyclical, *Populorum Progressio*, which can be read in such a way as to make room for use of revolutionary violence "where there is a manifest, long-standing tyranny which would do great damage to fundamental personal rights and dangerous harm to the common good of the country."[7] Roman Catholic ethical doctrine has always permitted violence in a "just war" and it has, under circumstances in which the Church has had a clear stake in revolutionary change, sanctioned revolutionary violence, including tyrannicide. However, especially since the French Revolution, the Roman Church has opposed revolutionary violence in most situations and today this opposition is very much emphasized at the Vatican level. On lower levels, most of all in Latin America, radical clergy and laymen in practice show a willingness to participate in revolutionary violence which undoubtedly greatly worries the higher ecclesiastical authorities.

On this whole matter of revolutionary violence it is hard to see how churches and theologians who have supported the use of military force in international war can take a position of absolute pacifism in the case of domestic revolutions. All the Christian moral sensitivity about the use of violence against persons should be active in both cases. So long as the veto against resistance to political authorities is withdrawn in those situations in which political authorities can be declared usurpers or tyrants or embodiments of basic disorder, the question of violence must be settled contextually in terms of the real alternatives that people confront. The distinction between overt and covert violence is most important here. The Uppsala Assembly report referred to declared that at times "law and order" may be a form of violence. The covert violence of those with power may at times have to be overcome by the overt violence of those who are their victims.

THE CONTEXT OF SOCIAL CHANGE: REVOLUTION OR REFORM?

One of the weaknesses of the current discussion of revolution in Christian circles is that it is insufficiently contextual (though Professor Shaull himself is an exponent of contextual ethics). Never, in his many discussions of revolutions, has he dealt with the real possibilities of revolution in any one place. What does he think about the resources for revolution in either of the countries in which he has been most involved, Brazil and the United States? Those two countries differ so much from each other that any generalizations about revolution applicable to one would almost certainly not apply to the other. He is right in insisting that at least the United

States should not prop up an oppressive regime in Brazil and that the people of Brazil should be allowed to have their own revolution. To wait for a revolution to take place in the United States in order to get a change in our policy in regard to Brazil would be to wait in vain; such a change might come as result of the determination of many Americans that there must be "no more Vietnams," not even in Latin America. But even the likelihood of such a change will probably depend on our particular responses to what takes place nation by nation in Latin America. Hopefully, the Christian community in the United States may be influenced in favor of greater openness to radical changes in Latin America as a result of the new radical Roman Catholicism in that continent. Such Catholic spokesmen may be able to provide a new type of communication to the minds and consciences of both Catholics and Protestants in this country. The erosion of religious anti-Communism that is taking place here may prepare the way for such communication. Is this a naive hope?

Professor Marcuse in his *Essay on Liberation* makes a useful distinction betwen a revolution and a revolt.[8] He regards the latter as possible in American cities; the word might also be used to describe the tumult on American campuses. In various recent writings he has denied the possibility of revolution in this country because the class of industrial workers which Marxist theory expects to be the bearer of revolution has too great a stake in the *status quo*. Actually, the rank and file of industrial workers and of their most likely white-collar allies are at present the bearers of the nation-wide movement for law and order. Most of the national leaders of organized labor may avoid racist politics, but they have been among the strongest supporters of the war in Vietnam and generally of an old-line anti-Communist foreign policy. Radical students and radical blacks cannot become the bearers of revolution against the forces of law and order backed not only by the police but by the world's greatest military establishment. Only a split in that establishment, with perhaps the air force op-

posing the army, or the CIA opposing the FBI, or some such
fantastic development, would make it possible to overcome
the power of the central government. The middle-class sym-
pathizers with the blacks and, to a lesser degree, with the students, are not inclined to illegal action, though many of
them would support limited forms of civil disobedience.
Barrington Moore makes his case very effectively against the
possibility of revolution in the United States, where both a
strong central government and the interdependence of urban
society would prevent the formation of "liberated areas" as
the bases for a revolutionary movement that might conceiv-
ably take power in the nation at large.[9]

American Christians should become open to the revolutionary impulses in the third world. They need not lecture
people who are in desperate need of revolutionary change
about the self-righteousness of revolutionaries, about the
failure of revolutionary utopian hopes, about the need of
judgment upon the new powers and the new society as well
as upon the old, about the danger that revolutionary violence
may become long-continued post-revolutionary terror. The
ecumenical community may, however, be a place where these
lessons are learned by Christians before it is too late. My own
fear is that too frequently the advocates of revolution will in
practice do no more than create situations in which there will
be no effective center of government and in which a succession of tumultuous events and civil wars may produce
political stalemate and economic stagnation. Such a fear, and
all the warnings against the abuses of power following revolutionary crises, should not close our minds to the possibility,
in some situations, of hopeful new beginnings growing out of
revolutionary struggles.

In the United States (assuming that a central revolutionary strategy cannot succeed in altering the location of power
or the political structure) political action for revolutionary
goals needs to be combined with creative responses to marginal
revolts. The riots that may take place in our cities according

to a familiar pattern are referred to here. A combination of many expressions of revolt against the war in Vietnam, some of them legal and some of them illegal, including the politics of protest represented by Eugene McCarthy and Robert Kennedy, brought down the administration of Lyndon B. Johnson. This was a remarkable achievement. I think that Professor Lochman, in his helpful warning that freedom of speech may not mean freedom to effect any real change, may still underrate the latter freedom in this country. The fact that we got Richard M. Nixon as President has probably disillusioned most of those who have taken part in the revolts, including the younger political activists who followed McCarthy and Kennedy. But Nixon knows that he cannot survive politically if he does not bring about real disengagement from Vietnam. Events have forced him to abandon the single-track anti-Communism on which he originally rode to power; as a result, under the pressure of a new world situation, he may be able as a conservative to effect a greater change of policy than would be possible for a left-wing Democrat. On the other hand, the bi-partisan political revolt in the Senate, not only against the Pentagon but against an interventionist foreign policy, will prove an important force. We should make the most of these political possibilities. The most unlikely people do learn from events; such people may be carried by unexpected situations into new policies which they would have rejected in advance.

I have spoken about creative responses to revolts. On a small scale, this may have occurred in some universities in relation to student revolts. New forms of governance have been created. Complicity with the war-making agencies of government has been radically reduced. Students will now be involved in educational planning as never before. Columbia and Harvard universities are taking a new look at the effects of their expansion on the community. This has already produced results that would probably not have come about without the student revolts.

The riots in the cities have had two effects: they have stimulated oppressive "law and order" movements, but they have also made the nation aware of the full extent of the failure of its institutions to make the cities liveable for the poor in general, and for the black and Puerto Rican minorities in particular.

We can expect more polarization in our society, and it will continue to be reflected by polarization in the churches. There is no revolutionary shortcut that can overcome this polarization by putting one of the parties to the polarization in full control. If there were, as of now it would probably be the wrong party! We must live and act in the hope that the real interest that most groups in the nation have in liveable cities and in peace, combined with the pressure of events and of social realities which are from time to time illumined by revolts, may create a new liberal-radical politics. The liberal factor would include both commitment to civil liberties and strong convictions based on reasonable interpretations of events and of social realities related to the necessary goals of justice and peace. The radical factor may not differ so much in content, but it may be more impatient, it may push harder, and it may sometimes inspire various forms of direct action to which I have applied the name "revolt." Such revolts will come out of sheer desperation. They may often be largely counterproductive. They cannot be the main force for political change. When they happen, those who would not initiate them may still interpret them so that they become a positive force for change. It is in this complex of influences and forces (which are far from being ideologically neat) that the radical Christian in this country must find his vocation.

THE INSTITUTIONAL CHURCH AND
REVOLUTIONARY CHANGE

The polarization in the churches is seen especially in the widespread rejection at the grass roots of the official teachings of denominations and ecumenical councils on social issues and of many of the political activities of the new breed of clergy. There are many laymen who agree with what the clergy have said and done about civil rights and about the war in Vietnam, but there has been a tendency for the laymen with power in local churches to take the other side or to try to avoid controversy in their churches. A recent study by Professor Jeffrey K. Hadden based on public opinion polls has shown the extent of this polarization. In the following passage he puts it into a theological context:

> The clergyman's new theology has moved him to express God's love in concern for the world, particularly the underprivileged, and in the desire to change structures of society which have ascribed to many a lower and disadvantaged status in life. The layman, on the other hand, seeks comfort and escape from the world in the sanctuary of God. He does not understand why ministers are not satisfied to restrict their concern to their own fellowship of believers, and to the extent that clergymen move outside their own flock, they pursue a collision course with the laity.[10]

After all allowances are made for the unfairness of any such generalization involving clergy and laymen, that passage does point vividly to a profound problem in our churches, both Protestant and Catholic. This volume would seem alien to a very large part of the Christian constituency. The situation has caused Professor Shaull almost to give up on the structures of the Church and to call for a new emphasis on small groups of true believers.

The difficulty with this new sectarian emphasis, with placing one's hope chiefly in small "paradigmatic communities," as Professor Shaull calls them, is that a large part of the prophetic stimulus within the Church comes from initiatives that would be impossible apart from the structures and agencies of the larger church, denominational and ecumenical. One basic reason for this is that the overview that comes from this ecumenical experience liberates people from uncriticized provincial and national outlooks. The 1966 Geneva Conference is an illustration of what is meant. This was an event of considerable influence in producing an awakening to a radical social responsibility on the part of many Christians throughout the world. It gave encouragement to paradigmatic groups that do exist. It prepared the way for the Uppsala Assembly of the World Council and on almost all important social issues the Assembly, an official body, gave support to the teachings that came from the unofficial Geneva Conference. (It was called officially, but charged to speak unofficially.) Many churchmen in North America and Europe felt for the first time the pressure of fellow Christians in Latin America and in other parts of the third world for revolutionary change. Indeed, in recent years the World Council of Churches has become in considerable measure a sounding board for churches in the third world. None of this kind of stimulus would be possible if it were not for these ecumenical structures that are themselves supported by denominational structures.

It was the initiatives of Pope John XXIII and the Vatican Council that opened windows, as the Pope said, in the Roman Catholic Church. These highly official initiatives emancipated Catholics all over the world from the effects of the rigid theological and moral teaching that had been previously supported by the Church's official structures. Pope Paul VI and the Roman Curia have caused much frustration among those who felt liberated by the Council; yet they cannot overcome the remarkable liberating effects of the Council among both clergy and laymen in most countries. There is today a great deal of theological and ecclesiastical confusion, but the old bland conformity cannot be restored. This applies to the issues of peace and race, to new approaches to Communism, and especially to the struggles of the nations of the third world for economic development. Where such development involves revolutionary crises, radical Catholics will play important roles. The social encyclicals, especially *Mater et Magistra*, *Pacem in Terris*, and *Populorum Progressio*, will continue to inspire and encourage Catholics who see the need of radical change in their countries.

There is and there will continue to be interaction among denominational and ecumenical leaders and structures, and voluntary groups of the kind that Professor Shaull emphasizes. Several years ago such a group was formed to oppose American policy in Vietnam. Known as "Clergy and Laymen Concerned About Vietnam," it has proved to be one of the most influential agencies working for peace in Vietnam and also for a revision of the foreign policy that led us into that disaster. From the beginning, this organization has had strong support from national denominational and ecumenical leaders. Without their help it would not have approached the national influence attributed to it. It has also had encouragement from important official agencies that saw it as moving in the same direction as they, but with greater freedom to act.

There is one recent and impressive example of how the institutions of the larger church can move ahead on an important controversial issue. The Council for Christian Social Action of the United Church of Christ prepared a resolution on amnesty for dissenters to the government's policy in Vietnam now in prison or in exile, to be acted on by the General Synod of the church that met in July 1969. This particular form of a much broader issue was relatively new and had not been widely discussed as such. The Council asked churches throughout the denomination to send messages to the Synod on this subject. The messages that came in from the churches ran about three to one against amnesty. After a long discussion, the Synod voted four to one for amnesty. This action can be interpreted, as Professor Ramsey would do in the light of his argument in his book *Who Speaks for the Churches?* as an example of unfair misrepresentation of the constituency of the churches.[11] I take it as an example of the way in which a new mind may be formed in the churches. When

amnesty is discussed locally it is likely to be rejected because
it goes against convictions formed on the basis of conventional
ideas of what constitutes patriotism and the citizen's responsibility to government. It is only when people have been
through an intensive process of discussion at a level of distinctively theological and ethical teaching, often against the background of world-wide ecumenical influences, that one can
expect support for anything as much against the grain of aver-
age opinion as amnesty. Many denominations can provide
similar illustrations of the same process, but this case is clear
cut. Councils of the church, regardless of the polity involved,
speak *to* rather than *for* their constituencies. What they teach,
and the policies and actions they initiate, are part of processes
by which the mind of the church may be changed. At present
there is strong opposition in many constituencies but, if the
church is to be more than a reflection of its cultural environment, the process must continue.

This process by itself is not enough. There are some common elements in two criticisms of contemporary Christian
activism and secularity already cited. There is the wistful
complaint by Marxists quoted by Professor Moltmann that
Christians should not lose sight of what they call "transcendence." There is the statement by Professor Hadden that the
layman "seeks comfort and escape from the world in the
sanctuary of God." I add a statement from Professor Thomas
O'Dea's sociological study of the alienation of youth. He says
that the articulate youth now engaged in rebellion "wish more
than anything else for what we have called an ontologically
grounded sense of direction." He says, "They seek meaning;
they seek it, to use their pet pejorative term, outside the 'establishment.'" Again: "They do not understand religion. But
they suspect that there is somewhere a realm that transcends
the sphere of everydayness — of work, huckstering, of war."[12]
These passages are quite different. The middle-class Christian's
desire that he not be reminded in church of the issues that
trouble him in the world, and his rejection of any radical

dealing with those issues in Christian terms, are, on the surface, far apart from the attitudes expressed in the other statements. Yet I think that the churches can only be true to their own message if they convey a meaning that involves both radical challenge and the grace that makes possible not escape but morale and healing.

When these are missing from the teaching of the churches, it is no wonder that there is rebellion, though the immediate form of the rebellion may seem very wrong. The radical challenge, even for those who at first welcome it, may produce only frustration without illumination concerning the deeper causes of the frustration, and without any mediation of the sources of morale and healing. The problem of socially radical theology and of the Christian groups guided by it is to avoid such a one-sided preoccupation with immediate social relevance that people are not helped to live with the usual human problems of pain and loneliness, of guilt and death, and have no resources with which to face the first disillusionments as they seek to respond to the prophetic message. To accept the radical challenge is to be true to the Church's essential calling. At the same time, such an approach may help to retain the loyalty of many of those who now reject that radical challenge. The Church should not try to hold loyalty by laying down this challenge; but neither should it assume in advance that it would do a great work in excluding such people; for they too may be changed — or, if not they, then their children — by the impact of both the Gospel and events.

NOTES

1. W. A. Visser 't Hooft, ed., *The First Assembly of the World Council of Churches: Official Report* (New York: Harper & Bros., 1949), p. 78.

2. Lambeth Conferences, "The Church and the Modern World" (Committee Report), Section on the Lameth Conference, 1948 (London: S.P.C.K.), Part 2, p. 21.

3. John C. Bennett, *Christianity and Communism* (New York: Association Press, 1948). This small volume was an attempt to state a dual view of Communism. It was written at the height of the Stalinist period and emphasized the responsibility to resist the extension of Communist power, viewing as the chief problem created by Communism its ideological and political absolutism. On the other hand the statement was made in it: "The errors of Communism are in large part the result of the failure of the Christians, and of Christian churches, to be true to the revolutionary implications of their own faith, that the effectiveness of Communism lies chiefly in the fact that it seems to offer the exploited and neglected peoples of the world what has been denied to them in a civilization that has often regarded itself as Christian" (p. 4.). In 1960, a later edition of this book was published under the title *Christianity and Communism Today*. It took account of the changes in the Communist world after Stalin's death. It will be republished with new material in 1970.

4. Jürgen Moltmann, *Religion, Revolution, and the Future* (New York: Scribner's, 1969), p. 64.

5. World Council of Churches, *Study Encounter*, vol. 4, no. 2, 1968.

6. Norman Goodall, ed., *Report of the Uppsala Assembly, World Council of Churches* (Geneva, 1968), section III, paragraph 15 (p. 48).

7. His Holiness, Pope Paul VI, *Populorum Progressio (On the Development of Peoples)* (Rome: The Vatican), paragraph 31.

8. Herbert Marcuse, *Essay on Liberation* (Boston: Beacon Press, 1969), p. viii.

9. Barrington Moore, "Revolution in America?" *The New York Review of Books* (January 30, 1969).

10. Jeffrey K. Hadden, *The Gathering Storm in the Church* (New York: Doubleday, 1969), p. 99.

11. Paul Ramsey, *Who Speaks for the Churches?* (Nashville: Abingdon Press, 1968), p. 41.

12. Thomas O'Dea, *Alienation, Atheism and Religious Revelation* (New York: Sheed and Ward, 1969), pp. 173–74.

2 *Religion in Radical Perspective*

THE RADICAL REFORMATION AND REVOLUTION
Franklin H. Littell

The tragedy of World War I, during which "Christian Europe," founded in the false Oikumene of the Holy Alliance at the Congress of Vienna in 1815, committed suicide, was followed by the agony of the church struggle with Nazism between 1933 and 1945, in which culture-religion in its most demonic form rose to challenge the gospel of Jesus Christ. These two events forced Christians to rethink their theology and their politics. In culture-religion, national or ethnic values dominate, so that a corrupted Word results; alternatively, a dead orthodoxy unrelated to life is perpetuated by rote. The false notion that right belief consists in the unilateral acceptance of ecclesiastical doctrine is allowed to prevail.

Nineteenth-century liberalism and the cultural and social values it baptized so uncritically were called into question

by men who passed through its schools, men who went
beyond both the old orthodoxy and the old liberalism. In
politics, men like Karl Barth, Josef Hromadka, Paul Tillich,
and Reinhold Niebuhr often used the insights of the "secular" prophets — Nietzsche, Marx, Freud — to break the chains
of a politics expressed in the language of ideas rather than in
the responsible uses of power. On the religious side, there
was a new encounter with the reformers and with the Bible
on which their confessions of faith were based.[1]

New editions and historical monographs resulted from
this encounter with the reformers. Specialized studies appeared, carrying both a lively dialogue with the past and a
vigorous handling of contemporary crises — such works as
Arthur C. Cochrane's in-depth analysis of the Confessing
Church's Confession of Faith at the Barmen Synod (1934),[2]
the most important confessional statement in many generations.

The renaissance of studies of Luther, Zwingli, Calvin,
Butzer — and, more recently, of the Catholic reformers whose
work was buried at the Council of Trent and proscribed by
the Index — was paralleled by yet another awakening of
scholarly effort which has been going on for decades but has
only recently come to wide attention. This line of effort, at
first historical but increasingly theological in import, is the
encounter with the "Left Wing of the Reformation," the
recovery of the contribution of the radical reformers. Growing numbers of contemporary Christian thinkers have come
to feel, with Günter Jacob, that the recent decades of misery
wrought by wars and totalitarian governments carry a clear
message for the Christian movement: "das Ende des kon-
stantinischen Zeitalters gekommen ist."[3] The message of the
Radical Reformation, which broke from the "magisterial
Reformation"[4] precisely at this point of interpretation of the
history of the Christian movement, has a relevance for all
who are disenchanted with the culture-religion of Victorian
England and the Wilhelminische Zeitalter, who seek to dis-

tinguish the Christian message from the particularisms of white European Christendom in decline.

This essay is directed to the body of material dealing with the Radical Reformation, much of it virtually unknown until this generation of monographs and edited sources, material which is now attracting the attention of both Protestant and Catholic scholars in growing number.[5] There are basic teachings, some of them now accepted in large sectors of the ecumenical fellowship, which were originally brought forward by the "heretics" (read "radicals") of the sixteenth century. As research and writing continues, there is coming into outline a Free Church movement covering five centuries of church history and suggesting a "third force" in contemporary Christianity parallel to traditional Protestantism and Catholicism. The line runs from the sixteenth-century Anabaptists, through radical Puritanism and Pietism, to the Wesleyan revival, the Great Awakening, the Great Century of Christian Missions. Its present strength is manifest in the churches of North America, with their voluntaryism, pluralism, and ecumenicity, in the younger churches of the former mission fields (so much closer to the congregations to which Paul wrote his epistles than they are to fifteen hundred years of "Christendom") and in the rapid growth of the "spirit-filled sects" in West Africa and Central America; even in the cities of Europe and North America.[6]

This "third force" can no longer be considered a marginal and somewhat bizarre footnote to mainline Protestantism, any more than the religious history of the United States can today be read as a short and aberrational appendix to European Christendom. The center of gravity has shifted in world Christianity; the principles for which Anabaptists and radical Puritans once suffered harassment and martyrdom are becoming common coin in the ecumenical dialogue: normative use of the New Testament and Early Church, pilgrim church, church covenant, church discipline, the congregation in mission, separation, voluntary membership, decision-making by consensus of all the faithful (lay co-determination), the integrity of conscience, church reunion, secular government. Emphasis upon the Christian peace testimony and upon believers' baptism are widespread, though not universal, among the Free Churches.

The most universal testimony has been against the "Constantinian era" and toward recovery of the religious liberty and voluntaryism of the early Church.

RELIGIOUS LIBERTY AND SECULAR GOVERNMENT

Religious liberty is basic to the advance of liberty and self-government, to the good of true religion, and to the health of the political order. Nothing corrupts churches or governments more consistently than that alliance of religious profession and governmental coercion by which politicians pretend to serve ultimate purposes in the exercise of political power. And nothing corrodes high religion more completely than the appropriation of the force of the state to serve ideological ends. Coercion of conscience is a poor foundation for church or state, as radical Protestantism has rightly maintained since the time of the Anabaptists of the sixteenth century — pioneers in the separation of the religious from the political covenants.

Thomas Jefferson, James Madison, and others who laid the foundations of the American experiment in liberty and self-government were clear that both the churches and the civil society benefited by a voluntary system of religious support. Nor was such conviction a party matter, although the New England Federalists came more reluctantly to acceptance of disestablishment. Harriet Martineau reported in this way her visit with Chief Justice John Marshall in 1835, emphasizing the stress he laid on the importance of religious liberty:

> *The first evening he asked me much about English politics, and especially whether the people were not fast*

> ripening for the abolition of our religious establishment,
> an institution which, after a long study of it, he consid-
> ered so monstrous in principle, and so injurious to true
> religion in practice, that he could not imagine that it
> could be upheld for anything but political purposes.[7]

On this matter, the wisest heads of the Democrats and the
Federalists agreed: liberty of conscience made for better
religion and sounder politics than any system of establishment.

Religious liberty implies both voluntary membership in
churches and secular government. Too little attention has
been given to the blessings of the latter,[8] although the mon-
strous ideological politics of culture lags, as represented, for
example, by the governments of Spain or Jordan, as well as by
the retrogressive policies of fascist and communist governments, should demonstrate the point. In the history of hard-
won human liberty, in struggling toward that level where
every human is respected in the dignity and integrity of his
person, nothing has been more important than the growing
awareness that the best government is secular: limited, a
human invention for specific purposes, "creaturely," in theological terms. Significantly, the lowest-grade religion and politics in America today is precisely that which is attempting
to take us back to "the good old days" of white, Anglo-Saxon,
"Christian" (read "Protestant") hegemony.

Now if the function of the state is thought to serve some
ideological purpose or other, including that of Christianity
misunderstood and misinterpreted as an ideology, radical
Protestantism is of another mind: against such government
its testimony has been either non-resistant or revolutionary.
But if government is modest in its claims and restrained in
its exercise of authority, both Anabaptists and radical Puritans have argued that it should be obeyed in all things lawful.
But coercion of conscience was not reckoned lawful.

Roger Williams uttered the religious condemnation of

established religion in his classic, *The Bloody Tenet of Persecuting:*

> *The blood of so many hundred thousand soules of Protestants and Papists, spilt in the Wars of present and former Ages . . . is not required nor accepted by Jesus Christ the Prince of Peace. . . . The Doctrine of persecution for cause of conscience is proved guilty of all the blood of the Soules crying for vengeance under the Altar. . . .*[9]

The goal was not, however, toleration — a practice quite consistent with established religion. As one of Isaac Backus' followers put the matter during the debate about New England's Standing Order:

> *Toleration is for the magistrate to say to us, "I will not give you the right to think and worship as you please, but I will wink at your violation of the law." Liberty is for you to say to me, "I shall believe and worship God according to the dictates of my own conscience, and I disclaim your right to impose, in these matters, any law upon me."*[10]

Religious liberty frees both church and state to fulfill their proper roles in human affairs, neither party corrupting or misusing the other for false purposes.

The elimination of religious or ideological parties' manipulation of political power and of government pretense of serving ultimate purposes has made headway in only a few countries to date. But it can fairly be said that whereas none of the major reformers approved separation and liberty, and Philipp of Hesse was the only ruler of his age (Catholic or Protestant) who refused to use the death penalty against "heretics" (i.e., dissenters),[11] the despised Anabaptists were in fact pioneers of modern understanding of the proper relationship of church and state.

Only those who understand the worth of secular government can appreciate the political contribution of Anabaptists and later Free Church men to political theory and practice. Not only is the position revolutionary in ecclesiological import, it is also revolutionary vis-à-vis the state. Although the principle of religious liberty has long been embodied in a fair Constitutional reading of the First Amendment, it has only recently been realized that secular government is as essential to liberty as is voluntary religion. Even in the present time, such reactionaries as Carl McIntire of the clerical radical right and the late Everett Dirksen, former senior Senator from Illinois, have commonly mixed backward-looking political programs with demands that government agencies further "Christian" interests for the sake of "Christian America." With reference to eastern Europe, where governments are made to serve Marxist ideological purposes, the case is equally clear: old-school thinkers champion "Christian" politics and ideology against Marxism, whereas the abler younger theologians fight for secular government. In most Muslim countries of the Middle East, where the religious establishment is as medieval as the economy is feudal, the same problem obtains: the alternative is not Christianity, misused in the Crusades and since then as an ideology, but rather, modern secular government.

Where governments are manipulated by religious or ideological caucuses and parties, the testimony of the Radical Reformation is revolutionary. Historically, it has ranged from refusal to bear arms and refusal to use the oath, to wider expressions of conscientious objection and to the illegitimate claims and uses of power by presumptuous governments. As the Socinians put it in the Racovian Catechism (1605): "Everyone has a right not to do things which he feels to be contrary to the will of God." The political inference leads directly to the Nürnberg Tribunal following World War II and to "selective conscientious objection." Far back of such advances in recognizing the integrity of the individual conscience, however, lies the essential first step: the freeing of churches from governmental control and the reduction of governments to the theological standing of "creatures."

Because of this deference to the conscientious concerns of every person, there has often been noted a peculiar affinity between constitutional government and democratic church order.

THE RADICAL REFORMATION AND POPULAR SOVEREIGNTY

"Participatory democracy," the sometime slogan of student radicals and black militants, stands in direct succession to the "prophesying" of radical Puritan "agitators." Under American federal and state constitutions (if they were loyally enforced), this principle would be conservative rather than revolutionary. The action of radicals is directed not so much to introduce new goals and change basic structures as to make effective the guarantees and rights which exist in principle but are not upheld in administration and legislation. If some bright and able students are shifting today to revolutionary ideology and action, their frustration and alienation are not directed against the American dream but against the American reality.

Nevertheless, in societies where the dignity, liberty, and integrity of every human are not yet recognized in constitutional theory — that is, under absolute monarchies and ideological dictatorships — the radical Protestant tradition still carries dynamite.

During the first period of Free Church history, the Anabaptists had no opportunity to work out a style of political responsibility. They lived under the death penalty and were often victims of the most savage cruelties "Christian" authorities could devise and "Christian" churchmen could rationalize. During the Commonwealth Period in England, however, radical Puritans had a chance to develop the political implications of the priesthood of all believers: voluntaryism and separation. Tielemann van Braght's *Martyrs'*

Mirror is the literary sign of the first period, John Milton's *Areopagitica* of the second.

In recent years various studies[12] have shown the way in which the town meeting emerged from the church meeting; with this, a certain style of decision-making was transferred from the religious to the political sphere. Oliver Cromwell himself was the "Lion of Judah" toward the enemies of the emerging English democracy, but "Lord Protector" of all dissenting sectaries. The process by which decisions were "talked up" until they became "the sense of the meeting" was practiced in Anabaptist circles, became classic among the Friends and other radical Protestants, and subsequently became a fundamental part of the English and other American constitutional tradition. Edmund Burke's reference to the House of Commons as a town meeting for all England derived from the earlier sectarian view, and so did the Atomic Energy Commission's decision-making procedures under David Lilienthal — where no votes were taken, but the chairman commonly summarized the prevailing consensus.

In old Christendom, emperors and kings ruled religious affairs just as they controlled military and political matters. Persons of political status dominated when they did not rule directly in the church. The floor plan of European cathedrals and chapels, with their reserved boxes for the nobility, illustrates the point. Among the Puritan meetings, however, all "worldly" authority stopped at the door of the meeting. The floor plan of the Spring Valley Meeting of Friends in Indiana or of the church at Amana (of Pietist origin) in Iowa makes the point clear: all believers sat among peers, in a square of benches, and none had precedence except as the Spirit gave utterance. Women too were encouraged to exercise the liberty of preaching.

Originally, the franchise was limited to persons of property. Not until the Great Reform Bill of 1833 in England, the abolition of slavery in the United States, and the American extension of the vote to women after World War I was the logic of popular sovereignty securely embedded in political practice. But the Tennessee Case of 1962, in which the Supreme 'Court enforced the premise of "one man, one vote," was entirely in line with the "secularization" of a decision-making process once limited to tiny societies of sectarian Protestants. The principle enunciated in the Port Huron Platform of Students for a Democratic Society (that human beings as persons, and without respect to social status or property, have the right to participate in making the decisions which govern their present and future) stands at the very center of 350 years of religious and constitutional development, as dangerous as that may sound to Strom Thurmond, Lester Maddox, James Eastland, and others of the "early seventeenth century." James Stuart was quite right at Hampton Court in 1605 when he rebuked the Puritans: "No bishop, no king!" Men who have learned to honor their neighbors and themselves in the thoroughly satisfactory discussion-toward-consensus of a congregational meeting will not for long submit to the indignities suffered by serfs or by subjects under despotisms.

Significantly, one of the major theoretical and practical programs of totalitarian regimes in reversing the movement toward representative government and secure citizens' rights is to smash all sub-political communities of independent leadership and purpose.[13]

CHRISTIAN REVOLUTIONARIES

All the radical reformers were primitivists,[14] interpreting church history on a scale marked Golden Age, Fall, and Restitution. Whereas the sign of the major reformers was *reformatio ecclesiae*, the sign of the radicals was *restitutio*. According to their particular bent, they gave differing qualities to the three ages. For the Anabaptists, the Golden Age was a time of heroic non-violent witness; the Fall occurred with the union of church and state under Constantine; the Restitution restored religious liberty and simple sermon-on-the-mount Christianity. For the anti-Trinitarians, the early church was inspired and free; the Fall came with the codification of dogma at Nicaea; the Restitution brought ethical religion to the fore and reduced the arid speculation of the theologians. For the Spiritualizers, the early church was without coercive structures; the Fall came with institutionalization and hierarchies; the Restitution restored spiritual fellowship among *alle guthertzige Leute*. Social revolutionaries like Thomas Müntzer, with a powerful drive for social and political righteousness, telescoped the Restitution of the True Church and the return to the Garden of Eden. Even among the quiet radicals, the return to the early church foreshadowed in some sense the eventual restoration of the creation to peace, brotherhood, and bountiful harvests. Among the revolutionaries, this dimension of the Restitution was a driving eschatological passion and led to violent revolt against the oppressors — bishops and princes.

For generations before the primary sources on Anabaptism became available, theologians and church historians of the established churches blamed the Peasants' War (1524–27) and the Münsterite episode (1534–35) on the radical reformers. Karl Holl, who saw in Thomas Müntzer the very prototype of Anglo-Saxon social Christianity, was a leader of this misinterpretation in the last generation.[15] But the truth is (and the documentary evidence is conclusive) that none of the Anabaptist groups — Swiss Brethren, South German Brethren, Hutterites, and Dutch Mennonites — hesitated to condemn violent revolution. They sympathized with the poor exploited peasants but condemned their turn to violence. Toward the teaching of the Davidic kingdom of John of Leiden and its radical Lutheran preacher, Bernt Rothmann, they were just as explicit. For this reason Social Democratic historians like Karl Kautsky and Belfort Bax have advanced the interpretation, perpetuated by some liberal contemporary historians also unfamiliar with the primary sources, that the Anabaptists were social revolutionaries until defeated, and that they then turned to pacifism out of a kind of "tired radicalism." In fact, however, Grebel and Marpeck and Huter and Menno were non-resistants (Matt. 5:39) from the beginning of their work, shunning the darker passages of Scripture in favor of the plain and simple Gospel, accepting persecution and suffering as the necessary lot of Christians at the end of the age.[16]

In the Radical Reformation itself there were numerous groupings and many individual prophets. Among them, these major typological categories can be discerned:

1. the Anabaptists, forerunners of religious liberty and the free churches;
2. Anti-Trinitarians;
3. Spiritualizers (anti-institutional and anti-creedal individualists like Sebastian Franck and Caspar Schwenckfeld);
4. social revolutionaries.

The mainline Anabaptists were non-resistants, opposed equally to war and revolution; their main contribution was in breaking the monolith of Christendom. Contemporary views of religious liberty owe much to them, and any theology of the secular must draw on their testimonies.

Thomas Müntzer introduced the eschatological note into active politics, but perished on the battlefield with the defeat of the peasants' forces.

For a few months in 1534–35, at Münster in Westphalia, the revolutionary craftsmen and peasants joined in ruling a city according to the views of religious revolution then current. Finally reduced by the combined Catholic and Protestant armies of Franz von Waldeck and Philipp of Hesse, for a few months the "Kingdom of David" at Münster was the scandal of Christendom.

The preacher of Christian revolution at Münster was Bernt Rothmann (c.1494–1535), like Thomas Müntzer a disciple of Martin Luther who grew impatient with a Reformation which left old political and economic structures intact. Rothmann was convinced that the corruption of

Christendom was so complete that only a total disruption could usher in the New Age. In his "Book of Wrath" of October 1534 he called upon all the common people to revolt against their religious and political rulers, to slay the godless, and to join with those who were erecting at Münster a Universal City. The new seal of the city adopted by the revolutionaries displayed a globe, surmounted by a cross and transfixed by a sword.[17]

First, Christian communism was reestablished in imitation of the Church at Jerusalem. Then the ingathering of "Israel" was to take place at Münster, accompanied by persecution of the faithful by the powers of the dying age. A just kingdom was to be established at the "New Jerusalem": Münster. This kingly universal city was to serve as a model for the imminent world regime.[18] Throughout the Lowlands and the German states the call aroused great excitement. Prophets arose and parties were formed. Thousands streamed toward Münster, although most of them did not get through the cordons established on the borders by the various governments.

The question at what point long-suffering (Geleidzamkeid) was to be abandoned and the slaying of the godless to begin was at first unclear. But when Münster was placed under siege the prophets recognized the signs and called upon the faithful to let fall the gentle yoke of Christ and pick up the harness of David to do Holy War. Those engaged in sorties against the besiegers sang psalms as they went forth to their deaths. When the city was finally taken, the leaders were tortured and their broken bodies hung in iron cages on the cathedral tower. When Henry Dosker visited Münster in the early 1920s to collect material for his book on the radicals, a few pieces of white bone could be discerned in the cages which still hung there, after four centuries, as a warning against religious revolution.

The revolutionaries at Münster have remained a whipping boy for churchmen throughout the generations. Yet their

teachings are worthy of reflection. They totally rejected
Christendom and its power structures. They believed the
total disruption of the present system was imperative and
inevitable. They turned to violence as a legitimate tool of
the faithful, authorized by Old Testament examples and by
the returning Messiah — Jesus Christ, who shall come to
judge the world. Their dialectic of history was completed in
a restitution of the true church, followed by a restoration
of the created order to its original perfection in communism,
pacifism, and enjoyment of a bountiful earth by all creatures.

Neither Müntzer nor the Münsterites were Anabaptists,
although the men of the establishment have sought to dis-
credit freedom of conscience and religious liberty by stress-
ing its occasional extremes. In a time of the breakup of
Christendom and its pretensions, however, in a time when
many structures of the ancient bondage are being sharply
challenged by revolutionaries of all types, the ideology of the
Christian revolutionaries of the sixteenth century is appro-
priately brought into the debate. They shared with other
contemporary radicals the vision of a restituted church and
a restored creation: their condemnation of oppression was
more complete and their choice of weapons more direct.

Of all the social revolutionaries, Thomas Müntzer was
the most interesting. In a recent study by Eric Gritsch there
is an excellent presentation of Müntzer's contribution and
its contemporary relevance.[19] Müntzer was not an Anabaptist,
but was termed that by those who tried to damn the non-
resistant *Täufer* by attributing all contemporary unrest to
their undermining the foundations of Christendom. Müntzer
was a radical reformer and a revolutionary, and his views are
therefore worth attention here.

Müntzer said that the "immaculate, virginal church became a prostitute shortly after the death of the apostles and
disciples."[20] The fault lay with those who then blocked free
access to the Holy Spirit for the common man: theologians,
bishops, monks. In the restitution he began at Allstedt in

Thüringia, he first reordered the worship of the parish with *The German Church Order*, *The German Evangelical Mass*, and *The German Church Order of Allstedt*. Then he founded a secret revolutionary society, the military League of the Elect, which was in due time to slay the godless and usher in a universal communist society based on Acts 2:44–45 and 4:32–35. Meeting official resistance, he preached inflammatory sermons condemning the ruling count, calling him a "heretical buffoon and rapacious oppressor"[21] and proclaiming that political power, as well as rule in the church, should be transferred to the common people. He announced the impending transformation of the world, with the end of history marked by visions, dreams, and ecstatic utterances. When the peasants arose in a vain effort to reclaim lost hunting, fishing, and grazing rights, he devoted himself to preparing them in military equipment and drill. The princes and professional soldiers slaughtered the peasants, and Müntzer died of the sword he had drawn. Under torture he signed two elaborate "confessions," which became the "sources" used by the establishment to make Müntzer the scapegoat of the Reformation.[22]

In recent years, the East German communist leaders have, in films and pamphlets, tried to make Müntzer the hero of the Reformation, contrasting him with the "bourgeois" Luther who betrayed the peasants.[23] In the dialogue with the past, it is imperative to listen as well as to speak; if we listen, we hear a different Müntzer from that of the myths of the establishment and communists. He was an indifferent organizer, an impatient leader, but one consumed by a great vision of justice, righteousness, and love for the common folk. That they loved him and followed him, at a time when most preachers and theologians were simply pensioners sitting at the gates of the wealthy and powerful and excusing their acts with proof-texts, is tribute enough. Neither Müntzer the scapegoat of the Reformation, nor Müntzer the hero of the Reformation is sustained in the primary sources.

Müntzer loved Joel and Daniel and quoted the dark passages extensively. In the Puritan Commonwealth, the Diggers and Fifth Monarchy Men also combined a religious and political eschatology. Some were like today's Jehovah's Witnesses, who suffer greatly because they refuse to fight for any worldly governments, but who will fight like the Lord's own legions in the final conflict. Others attempted immediate action. In either case, the program for a restitution of the true church is intertwined with the vision of a restored creation—a vision not dependent upon Joel and Daniel alone but powerfully presented in such New Testament passages as Colossians, 1:15ff. That the social revolutionaries preferred the Old Testament imagery has more to do with their rejection of the sweet yoke of Jesus and their picking up the rough harness of David to slay the godless oppressors (as Rothmann put it in his *Von der Wrake*, 1534).

Luther urged the people to read the Bible. Müntzer said the poor peasant couldn't buy a Bible and read when he had to work long hours every day in order just to eat. Luther said each should stay in his appointed calling (*Beruf*), sons following their fathers as knights, peasants, craftsmen, millers, woodworkers. To want to change was a sign of unfaithfulness. Müntzer was "upward mobile" himself, and looked for the day of the common man: there were no bishops, popes, theologians, counts, kings, or emperors in the Church at Jerusalem, none in Eden, and probably none in heaven either. Luther has been used frequently to sustain those who hold political power — even a man as diabolical and illegitimate as Hitler. Müntzer, although his language is forbidding, is much more interesting to revolutionaries.

AN UNDERGROUND RIVER

Müntzer, like the Zwickau prophets, received many of his working concepts during a visit to Prague. The tradition of the revolutionary Tabor spoke to his condition and made him a missionary of revolt. And the Taborites drew from a continuing western tradition of revolutionary eschatology.

For centuries there has been in existence in the west an underground river of anti-institutional force, sometimes exploding its banks within the church, and sometimes directly affecting politics. When Karl Marx wrote of the final withering away of the state, he drew from that river, although he was no more aware of the source than today's Pentecostals are when they proclaim the "Eternal Gospel" and announce the breaking in of the Age of the Spirit. The main source of this anti-structural and anti-creedal tradition, with its eschatology and revolutionary force, is Joachim of Fiore (c. 1132–1202).

Joachim, of whose work Ernst Benz of Marburg was the earliest and remains the fullest interpreter,[24] was an abbot and teacher whose students preserved his sayings: they surfaced during the struggle of the radical Franciscans against the pope and the conservatives. Basically, Joachim developed a triad system for interpreting the three periods of history. In the Age of the Father, men lived under the law; in the Age of the Son, under grace; in the Age of the Spirit, the church would wither away, and fear and faith would be superseded by love. The Fraticelli identified the papacy as the Anti-Christ because it refused to fade away at the end of the second period, as the Spirit was breaking in and informing believers directly. From Joachimitism, reappearing in Bohemia and Reformation Germany and Commonwealth England, and in various religious and political movements today, the periodization of history became an ideological weapon against the old and unyielding order.

In the past, Christian revolutionaries like Müntzer, Pfeiffer, Hans Hut, Gerard Winstanley, John Lilburne, and even Martin Luther King, Jr., have leaned heavily upon an interpretation of history which lends eschatological fervor and certainty to beliefs which would otherwise remain mere intellectual concepts. The great hymn of Louis Bourgeois:

Turn back, O Man, foreswear thy foolish way . . .
Earth shall be fair, and all her people one:
Nor till that hour shall God's whole will be done. . . .

conveys in familiar form the mood and conviction by which
the dream of Eden has from time to time surfaced as a program for the future. Even quiet, non-resistant Anabaptist/
Mennonites, who withdraw their support and participation
from regimes committed to luxury and war, serve a revolutionary purpose. Although they negate violent methods, their
work for restitution points toward an eventual restoration of
the created order.

Joachim was the first to integrate an idea of progress into
the view of history. Although his particular typology, and the
interpretation his various followers have given to Golden Age,
Fall, and Restitution, may not today commend themselves
to an analytical and critical age, the passion for the age of
justice, righteousness, mercy, and peace breaks out from time
to time in new forms. And in that season, a vision of past
glory combines with a present commitment to level moun-
tains and make crooked places straight. For the Anabaptists
and radical Puritans and those Free Church men who came
after them, a fallen Christendom is purified and straightened
by return to the True Church of the early days, and by the
elimination of all ultimate claims from the pedestrian business of politics.

The radical reformers, in their separation from state-
church establishments — "fallen," whether Protestant or
Catholic — had revolutionary impact upon both church and
state, an impact felt even more today, as men seek to replace a flaccid culture-religion with a church made up of a
pilgrim people of discipline and integrity. Parallel to this
cause, but separate from it, is the need to replace arrogant
governments with limited instruments controlled by the
truth that man, and man alone, is the yardstick by which all
finite institutions are measured.

NOTES

1. Friedrich Gogarten, "Theology and History," in Wolfhart Pannenberg et al., History and Hermeneutic (New York: Harper & Row, 1967), pp. 35f.

2. Arthur C. Cochrane, The Church's Confession Under Hitler (Philadelphia: Westminster Press, 1962).

3. Gűnter Jacob, "Der Raum fűr das Evangelium in Ost und West," in Bericht űber die außerordentliche Synode der evangelischen Kirche in Deutschland, 1956 (Hannover: Evangelische Kirchenkanzlei, 1956), pp. 17–29.

4. George H. Williams, The Radical Reformation (Philadelphia: Westminster Press, 1962), Introduction.

5. Franklin H. Littell, The Origins of Sectarian Protestantism (New York: Macmillan Co., 1958), first published by the American Society of Church History in 1952; Donald F. Durnbaugh, The Believers' Church (Elgin, Ill.: Brethren Publishing House, 1969). On Catholic interest, see Michael Novak, "The Free Churches and the Roman Church," Journal of Ecumenical Studies 2 (1965): 426–47; Daniel O'Hanlon, "What Can Catholics Learn from the Free Churches?" in Hans Kűng, ed., Do We Know the Others? (New York: Paulist Press, 1966), pp. 94–103.

6. Cf. for example Walter J. Hollenweger, Enthusiastisches Christentum (Zűrich: Zwingli Verlag, 1969).

7. Allan Nevins, ed., American Social History as Recorded by British Travellers (New York: Henry Holt & Co., 1923), p. 189.

8. Franklin H. Littell, "The Secular City and Christian Self-restraint," in The Church and the Body Politic (New York: Seabury Press, 1969), chap. 6.

9. S. H. Smith et al., eds., American Christianity (New York: Charles Scribner's Sons, 1966), pp. 152–53.

10. Quoted in Daniel B. Ford, New England's Struggle for Religious Liberty (Philadelphia: American Baptist Publication Society, 1896), p. 184.

11. Franklin H. Littell, Landgraf Philipp und die Toleranz (Bad Nauheim: Christian Verlag, 1957), pp. 32f.

12. A. D. Lindsay, The Essentials of Democracy (Philadelphia: University of Pennsylvania Press, 1929); Daniel T. Jenkins, Church Meeting and Democracy (London: Independent Press, 1944).

13. Otto Kirckheimer, "In Quest of Sovereignty," The Journal of Politics 6, no. 2 (1944): 139–72.

14. Franklin H. Littell, "Primitivismus," in Franklin H. Littell and Hans Hermann Walz, eds., Weltkirchenlexikon: Handbuch der Ökumene (Stuttgart: Kreuz Verlag, 1960), cols. 1182–87.

15. Karl Holl, "Luther und die Schwärmer," in Gesammelte Aufsätze zur Kirchengeschichte (Tűbingen: J. C. B. Mohr, 1923), 1:420–77.

16. On the general matter of the interpretation of Anabaptism, see Franklin H. Littell, "The Changing Reputation of the Anabaptists," in The Origins of Sectarian Protestantism, chap. 5.

17. Franklin H. Littell, Origins of Sectarian Protestantism, pp. 29–32.

18. C. A. Cornelius, Die Niederländische Wiedertäufer während der Bela-

gerung *Münsters 1534 bis 1535* (Munich: Kaiserl. Akademie, 1869), p. 12.

19. Eric W. Gritsch, *Reformer Without a Church: The Life and Thought of Thomas Muentzer* (1488?–1525) (Philadelphia: Fortress Press, 1967).

20. Eric W. Gritsch, *Reformer Without a Church*, p. 57.

21. *Ibid.*, p. 82.

22. *Ibid.*, chap. 6.

23. *Ibid.*, pp. 162f.

24. Ernst Benz, *Ecclesia Spiritualis* (Stuttgart: Kohlhammer Verlag, 1934); also, *Evolution and Christian Hope* (New York: Doubleday & Co., 1966), chap. 3.

FROM PASSIVE TO ACTIVE MAN: REFLECTIONS ON THE REVOLUTION IN CONSCIOUSNESS OF MODERN MAN

John C. Raines

In his book *Cosmos and History* Mircea Eliade gives this intriguing description of the predicament of man today.

> Modern man can be creative only insofar as he is historical; in other words, all creation is forbidden him except that which has its source in his own freedom; and, consequently, everything is denied him except the freedom to make history by making himself. [Yet] the more modern he becomes — that is, without defenses against the terror of history — the less chance he has of himself making history.[1]

Eliade is pointing to the transformation of modern man from a passive to an active understanding of himself in relation to the world, and the frustration of this new consciousness under the conditions of modern society. The intent here is to examine this idea and some of its implications for the western Christian tradition.

The question to be examined is not human activity as such. It is taken for granted that man has always in fact been active toward his environment, transforming the world in which he finds himself to suit his various projects. Rather, the problem of the title is man's *understanding* of himself in relation to this activity. Does he view himself as an active creator of his human world or as a passive imitator of some higher transcendent order or orderer? How does he "know" himself vis-à-vis the given universe of reality and his transformation of this reality through his own activity? In short, the problem dealt with is the problem of man's *consciousness*, his way of living with and interpreting himself in the world.

This thesis follows Eliade's — namely, that to pose the question in this way is to reveal a fundamental change in consciousness from man of traditional society to man of advanced or incipient industrial society. Contemporary man, insofar as he knows himself as contemporary, is in process of coming home to *himself* in a *human* world, rather than finding this world a product of some other and therefore alien activity — of "nature," let us say, or of "divine sovereignty," or perhaps of "reason." He is discovering that the content of these supposedly supra-human ideas, concepts, powers is in fact his own human activity — his own product, of which in his self-forgetfulness he has become a product. Consequently, his posture toward the given cosmos of reality is active, self-transcending, and dialectical rather than passive or organic. This seems to be the most fundamental "ought" modern man speaks to himself among his many other ought and duty-speakings.[2]

We shall argue that this transformation to active consciousness is an increasingly accurate description of the present situation, despite abundant evidence that man continues also to flee the exposure and unprotectedness of this new self-perception. This revolution in consciousness requires of the religious approach to life a fundamental reevaluation of its tradition. We shall touch upon this more general problem, however, only as it relates to our immediate concern with the religious thought of western Christianity.

The analysis can be clarified and focused with a brief description of the self-understanding of traditional man, that interpretation of his being-in-the-world from which modern man is now in process of emigration.

THE CONSCIOUSNESS OF TRADITIONAL MAN

In recent years there has developed an impressive unanimity among scholars of varying disciplinary interests concerning the world-view of traditional man. Ancient Near Eastern studies have been especially helpful in this regard. Eric Voegelin summarizes this material in his concept of "the cosmological form of civilization" which typified the archaic self-understanding. He points to the predominance of the myth of *cosmic participation* as the peculiar way in which traditional man experienced himself in the world. As Voegelin puts it:

> The great stream of being, in which he flows while it flows through him, is the same stream to which belongs everything else that drifts into his perspective.[3]

It was in terms of this socially fundamental image of *participation* that man of the Ancient Near East defined his situation, organizing a significant universe, creating for himself a familiar and understandable place, a world.

Under this form of consciousness man receives his life as meaningful precisely because, and only to the extent that, it participates in and reproduces the cosmic totality. His way of being in the world is as an imitation and repetition of this

more transcendent and universal Whole. He knows himself
and his action not as his own but as re-presentations of the
powers, gods, and laws that rule and order the cosmos. For
archaic man, *to be* means to be passive, to maintain one's
harmonious integration in the cosmic coherence. And to be
good means the perfecting of this imitation and conformity.
Henri Frankfort confirms this picture in his description of
the social role of the sacred monarch. "The ancients," he
points out:

> experienced human life as part of a widely spreading net-
> work of connections which reached beyond the local and
> the national communities into the hidden depth of nature
> and the powers that rule nature. . . . Whatever was sig-
> nificant was imbedded in the life of the cosmos, and it
> was precisely the king's function to maintain the harmony
> of that integration.[4]

For traditional man it is this cosmic mediation which is the
very substance of legitimacy and sovereignty, the re-produc-
tion of the *polis* as an imitation of the cosmos. He "knows"
society not as a product of his own human activity but as a
microcosm of the macrocosm, as a *cosmo-polis*.

This same self-understanding and consciousness can be
found in the Greek city-state, with its socially fundamental
ideal of the repetition of the exemplary models, the paradig-
mic "acts of greatness," of the founding heroes.[5] Here again
man interprets his way of being in the world not as *his own*
way and action but as an imitation of more primordial and
universal archetypes. His relationship to his given universe
of reality is passive. Greek philosophical idealism did nothing
to alter this traditional consciousness. Indeed, it but ab-
stracted from it in order to set it on a less crudely mythical
and more "rational" basis in face of the skeptical attacks of
the Sophists. Thus Plato asserts that it is only true philosophers (i.e., metaphysical idealists) who can "sketch the
ground-plan of the city"; for they alone can see the original

and copy it, by "letting their eyes wander to and fro from the model to the picture, and back from the picture to the model."[6] Eliade correctly perceives in this the ideological justification of traditional consciousness. As he says: "the Platonic doctrine of Ideas was the final version of the archetype concept, and the most fully elaborated."[7]

To summarize, traditional man does not know the world as a human world, a product of his own productivity. In the midst of his action he does not know himself as active, and so he becomes a product of his original production. He passively imitates himself, while assuming he is rehearsing the divine verities, universal rational insights, laws of nature, and so on. This fact of dwelling passively within himself and the given cosmos of reality does not arise as a conscious problem for him, because traditional consciousness has already occupied his field of understanding. It is the lens, so to speak, through which he views and receives his life. Indeed, the very fact that we can state this problem today, and perhaps be understood in stating it, indicates that modern man has indeed passed beyond this traditional mode of being, and is moving now from a passive to an active consciousness of himself in relation to the world.

THE DOMINANCE OF PASSIVE MAN IN CHRISTIAN THOUGHT AND CIVILIZATION

Given this modern revolution in consciousness it would be convenient for theologians and apologists to assume that western Christianity is, if not actually responsible for this change, at least basically friendly to it. Unfortunately, the overwhelming weight of historical evidence refutes this assumption. It was not from the Sophists or classical materialists that Christianity learned its philosophy and produced the world-hypothesis within which it could explain its faith and define its situation in the world. Rather it was, as we know, in Greek idealism that Christianity found the educator of its consciousness: especially in Neo-Platonism and Stoicism.[8] The process by which the early church produced its ethic of sex illustrates how pervasive this influence was at the level of early Christian consciousness.

The New Testament community had certain rules of thumb to regulate the sexual relations of their congregants. But it had little in the way of a systematic, theoretical ethic by which to "explain" these household virtues.[9] With the delay of the parousia and the new missionary enterprise to the gentile world, this became an increasing embarrassment. Contrary to popular notions, the early church generally opposed the radical devaluation of "incarnate" existence evidenced in Gnosticism and the widely appealing mystery cults. Over against this world-dualism, the early apologists sought a way of theoretically saying "yes" to man's life in the body.

They found their desired "ethic" — that is, theoretical model of order and legitimation — in Stoicism, which viewed the world positively as a unified and hierarchical order of ends and values up to the fullness of Good, the *summum bonum*. It was from this Stoic vision of the teleological *world-Nous* that Christianity took its fundamental image of explanation and defined its situation in the world. Here was a theoretical way for the Church to say "yes" to man's incarnate existence, but "yes" after a particular shape and form. All sex, for example, was now understood to be licit that adhered to its proper end or *telos* in the overarching cosmos of ends. Its obvious end was procreation. What, then, was obviously illicit sexually (abortion and contraception) was whatever interrupted this legitimating, end-orienting cosmic coherence. Thus the early church succeeded in defining its situation in the world, explaining systematically how and why man's life in the body (among other things) was morally acceptable. It had produced its needed social ethic.

But did the early church understand itself as so producing? Did it recognize in this world-hypothesis the activity and production of man? Was its consciousness active or passive? It seems evident that it was the latter. The Church understood itself as discovering the universal "laws of nature" when in fact it was discovering the intellectuality and consciousness of Greek idealism. It was this world-view and consciousness that the early Christian community accepted as its own. Christian man, no less than archaic or classical man, knew his activity in the world as not his own but an imitation and repetition of the actions of a transcendent and supra-human order and orderer. His posture toward the established universe of reality was fundamentally passive.

Given the limits of this presentation, we will not be able to follow in a detailed way the career of this passive consciousness in its development and dominion throughout Christian civilization. We must be satisfied with indicating its overwhelming presence in certain critical periods and thinkers.

Saint Augustine is justly referred to as "the father of western theology." He is, to be sure, a complex and in many ways contradictory and unfinished thinker. In no area of his theology is this more evident than in his conception of the Christian's relationship to the world. The opposition between the *civitas dei* and the *civitas terrenae* is fundamental and unresolved, except above history in the mystery and beatitude of divine wisdom. Nevertheless, the Christian's task remains, as Augustine says, "to make the peace of the heavenly city bear upon the peace of this earth." If we inquire into the means by which this task is to be accomplished we encounter a familiar intellectual image and consciousness.

Those who are fond of quoting Augustine's "love, and then do what you will" — and thus cite the Doctor of Grace as the first of the new moralists — fail to observe that Augustine qualifies this idea by speaking of an "ordered love." "Virtue," says the saint, "is well-ordered love."[10] And the structure of this order is the hierarchical gradation of being. "All natures," he says, inasmuch as they are, and have therefore a rank and species of their own, and a kind of internal harmony, are certainly good. And when they are in the places assigned to them by the order of their nature, they preserve such being as they have received. And those things which have not received everlasting being, are altered for better or for worse, so as to suit the wants and motions of those things to which the Creator's law has made them subservient, and thus tend in the divine providence to that end which is embraced in the general scheme of the government of the universe.[11]

It is by loving God, who is the Fullness of Being — and as such alone worthy of our devotion — that we receive "rightly ordered love" (*dilectio ordinata*); on the other hand, by loving something outside of its proper placement in this hierarchy of being, our love becomes disordered and sinful (*dilectio inordinata*). Indeed, it is the very essence of pride or *superbia* to relate ourselves to the world apart from its participation and proper location in this cosmic continuum of being. As Christians, we "know" our activity in and toward the world as meaningful and good, not as it is in itself — that is, *as human activity* — but as an imitation, repetition, and conformity to the hierarchical *Logos* of Being. This is our proper "imitation of Christ," which ethic is, in turn, the principle effect of the world-defining function of *Logos Christology*. For Augustine, man's relationship to the world, and his consciousness in this regard, remain essentially passive. Our activity as Christians is to be the acting out of this *imitatio* and *humilitas*.

However, this theme of classical idealism remains submerged in Augustine under the weight of his much more pervasive world pessimism and his preoccupation with the salvation and heavenly ascent of the soul above this general disaster. It was only in later centuries, when new historical circumstances made it possible to move beyond the eternal opposition of the "two cities" and revive again the ancient hope of a Universal Monarchy and Religion, that the implications of this idealistic theme, and the consciousness on which it was founded, could be fully elaborated and made socially effective. For this, we must turn to the period of the Investiture Controversy and the understanding of man projected in high Scholasticism.

Ernst Troeltsch, in his brilliant treatise on *The Social Teaching of the Christian Churches*, warns against treating the history of Christian thought as a pure "dialectic of ideas." Ideas emerge, he indicates, out of a fundamental conversation with the social, economic, and political circumstances of the world. Thus, Troeltsch maintains that the ideational content of High Scholasticism developed, and could only develop, in response to certain prior changes in the social and institutional circumstances of the medieval world: (1) the experience of the Territorial Churches; (2) the rise of the imperial ambitions of the Carolingian monarchs; and (3) the attempt of the Gregorian popes to regain centralized control over the ecclesiastical bureaucracy.[12] It was out of the interplay of these concrete historical circumstances, with the Augustinian intellectual heritage, that the medieval world-view was produced. That is to say, the idea of a universal *corpus Christianum*, a Christianized Church-State, arose as much from the altered circumstances of the social and political world as from the internal ideational development of the dogma of the Church.

With the breakdown of the political bureaucracy of the Roman Empire, the churches of the trans-Alpine became ever more firmly dominated by the territorial princes and lords. The reason for this was practical and political. It was only the clergy during this period who possessed the requisite skills of writing and general administrative ability for routinized, bureaucratic control. With the rise of the imperial

vision of the Carolingian monarchs, such a network of political bureaucracy became a fundamental practical necessity and
the ecclesiastics were co-opted. As Lord Bryce has put it:

> Bishops were princes, the chief ministers of the sover-
> eign, sometimes even the leaders of their flocks in war;
> kings were accustomed to summon ecclesiastical councils
> and appoint ecclesiastical offices.[13]

It was, in short, out of this concrete human activity in
the world that the "two cities" of Augustine lost their
strangeness to each other, were practically intermingled and
finally ideologically transformed into the unified vision of the
single *corpus Christianum.* The radicalness of this transformation in world-perception is strikingly illustrated by these
words from the twelfth-century canonist, Stephen of Tournai.
He used the language of Augustine's "two cities" to reverse
their original opposition and intent. "In the same city and
under the same King," he said:

> there are two peoples and corresponding to the two peo-
> ples two ways of life, corresponding to the two ways of
> life two authorities, and corresponding to the two authori-
> ties two orders of jurisdiction.

Thus far Augustine; but then Tournai continued:

> The two peoples are the two orders in the Church,
> the clergy and laity. The two ways of life are the spiritual
> and the secular, the two authorities are the priesthood and
> the kingship, the two jurisdictions are the divine and
> human laws. Give each its due and all things will agree.[14]

The two cities of Saint Augustine have become two juris-
dictions within the one city of the universal *Ecclesia,* whose
single king and earthly head is the *vicarius Christi,* the
papacy.

As we have said, this vision of a universal *corpus Christianum* was learned first of all not from the "unchanging

Mind of the Church" but from the mundane activity of man
in the world. Harnack points this out.

> The Church only developed her aggressive character
> after Charlemagne had shown her how the vicarius
> Christi should reign on earth. Nicholas I learned from
> Charles I; and the Gregorian Popes learned from Otto I,
> Henry II, and Henry III, how the rector ecclesiae should
> exercise his office.[15]

But neither the Church nor the world knew itself as so
learning. On the contrary, medieval man understood this new
definition of his situation in the world as an eternal and universal Idea and Ideal, a reality and necessity passed down
from a Transcendent Realm where alone it was fully realized.
As Gierke points out, during the High Middle Ages

> Christendom, which in destiny is identical with Man-
> kind, is set before us as a single, universal Community,
> founded and governed by God Himself. Mankind is one
> "mystical body"; it is one single and internally connected
> "people" or "folk"; it is an all-embracing corporation
> (universitas), or, with equal propriety, the Common-
> wealth of the Human Race (respublica generis humani).[16]

This Ecclesia is understood as a mystical entity and unity,
existing as a "real substance" outside of the world of particulars. It is on a level with the species and genera which alone
have true reality. Like Plato's Ideal, it is a society which is
essentially situated in heaven, receiving a mystical identity
and personality as the unum corpus Christi. Its material
existence on earth is, and can only be, a repetition and re-
presentation of this heavenly Reality.[17]

So it happened that out of his human material and
mental activity in the world man produced an altered consciousness, a new universe of reality. But he did not know
himself as so producing. In relating to himself by way of self-
forgetfulness he lost hold of the world as his own world and

became a product unconsciously produced by his original material and ideational productions. The theology of Thomas Aquinas did not alter in any essential way the passivity of this medieval self-understanding and consciousness.

Once again, we need remind ourselves that behind Saint Thomas lies not only the developing dialectic of ideas but also the altering circumstances of the world — that is, not only Aristotle but a waning feudalism and rising mercantile culture. As Ernst Troeltsch points out, the fundamental categories of Aquinas' theology — universality, subsidiarity, organicism, and patriarchalism — are in many ways but the mundane realities of the feudal manor and medieval town Writ Large.[18] It remains true, however, that it is only modern man who is provoked to recognize such facts, and the interpretation which follows from such a recognition — and this out of a consciousness of himself in the world that is radically different from that of his medieval forebears.

The degree to which Aquinas partook of the passive consciousness of traditional man is illustrated in a passage from *Summa Theologica* II-II, q. 42, where he was talking about "sedition." In the course of his argument he used a quotation from Augustine on Cicero's definition of the *respublica* as a "rational compact of justice." He was, without noticing it, considerably less pessimistic about the metaphysical competence of natural reason than Augustine.[19] He based this optimism on a distinction, originally produced by Irenaeus, between the "image of God" (*imago Dei*) and the "likeness of God" (*similitudo Dei*). While the latter has been completely lost in the Fall, the former — the rational image — has survived relatively intact. This gives to natural man, as he operates within the co-natural limits of the world, a certain independence from the precipitous imposition of ecclesiastical reality and authority.[20] But just how relative this independence in fact is, and indeed how inconsequential in terms of the questions that interest us here, is made clear when Thomas defines the *operation* of this "natural reason." "All knowledge of truth," he argues, "is but an irradiation of and participation in the Eternal Law."[21] Indeed, the "rational proofs" of God's existence which begin the Summa depend entirely upon the efficacy of precisely such an analogia entis.[22]

It is plain, in short, that Aquinas remains a moderate Realist and not a moderate Nominalist. To the realists, man does not discover himself in his rational activity but a participation in and repetition of another, higher and more "real" realm. For Thomas too, man knows himself most truly when he knows himself as integral to a cosmic commonwealth transcending the world of particulars even while incorporating them as their final end and cause. Man understands himself in his full reality not as he is in himself but as a receptive participant in the universal, mystical body of Christ, the cosmic corpus Christianum, the Ecclesia.

Thus in his human ordering activity in the world, medieval man does not recognize himself in his action but the imitation and repetition of another. In the name of both faith and reason, in the name of God and of Nature, medieval man does not notice himself as the namer. As rational man, as natural man, and as religious man he forgets himself and becomes passively defined by that which he originally defined. His consciousness remains traditional and passive.

The Reformation was not to change this fact. This becomes especially evident in the reformed corpus Christianum projected in Calvin's Institutes — that manual of true piety and propriety which was to play so dominant a role in the Protestanism of Great Britain, France, and the United States. Bohatec refers to the abiding "pathos for order" that moved and agitated the depths of the Genevan reformer. For Calvin, reformation was to mean precisely what it says: the reformation of the entire religious and moral life of the Christian person and society. Christianity and confusion were mutually exclusive terms, as contradictory as God's order and man's disorder, as obedience and self-will. The reformer's quest for the true order of order led him beyond the synthesis of reason and revelation attempted in extreme and moderate realism and in the "Christian philosophy" of the Paris humanists. Indeed, Calvin became persuaded that reason, when it concerns itself with matters of God and salvation, is not only "blinder than a mole" but in this blindness becomes "a perpetual forge of idols."[23] Man falls in love with the imaginings of his own heart under the guise of his ostensible love for and rational ascent toward God. The stubbornness of this covert self-will and pride must be broken and man revealed to himself in his utter insufficiency and dependence upon God. It was after this fashion that Calvin referred to his own first steps in faith as *"a sudden conversion to docility."*[24] Emptied of self, the Christian can then be ordered to the order of God, as regards both his justification and his regeneration. Whereas reason and merit led only to the disaster of pride and self-will, Word and Spirit (Revelation) lead to "the sure and certain knowledge of God" and humble "conformity" to what thus is known.[25]

The result, to be sure, is a supremely active life in and toward the world. Calvin understood the Christian life not as "a vessel filled with God" but as an active "tool and instrument" of the Divine initiative.[26] But this is precisely our point. Active toward the world, the Christian knows himself as utterly passive and obedient toward God, whose Will it is his sole task to discover and obey. In the reformer's own words,

> The glory of God peculiarly shines forth in human nature where the mind, will and all the senses represent the divine order.[27]

So it happens that the reformed saint, no less than the medieval saint, does not recognize *himself* in his activity but the passive reception and imitation of the activity required by some other, supra-human power, law, and will. In his human productivity he does not recognize his production as his own.

Calvin, it should be noted, is characteristically blunt on this point. "We are not our own," he proclaims,

> let not our reason nor our will, therefore, sway our plans and deeds. We are not our own; let us therefore not set it as our goal to seek what is expedient for us according to the flesh. We are not our own: in so far as we can, let us therefore forget ourselves and all that is ours. . . . Let this therefore be the first step, that a man depart from himself in order that he may apply the whole force of his ability in the service of the Lord.[28]

From the perspective of our interests now, it is difficult to imagine a less ambiguous proclamation of the passive consciousness of traditional man. In his responsive action in the world, man does not know he is responding to himself and is, in this sense, humanly active and responsible. In understanding his actions as conformity to the activity of God (or Nature or Reason) he does not know himself in his interaction with the world as in conformation with (or in revolution against!) his own human activity. He knows himself instead as "obedient" (or "natural" or "rational"). The definer, in short, has become the defined. Man knows himself as "not his own." Precisely!

Such, in part, is the career of passive man and his dominion in western Christian thought and civilization — and indeed beyond it. We turn now to the revolution of consciousness which occurs with man's passage from this passive to an active understanding of himself in relation to the world — which is to say, his passage to a *dialectical* definition of his situation vis-à-vis the given universe of reality.[29]

FROM PASSIVE TO ACTIVE MAN

There have been many attempts to locate so-called watersheds in the evolution of western civilization. Where one

discovers these tends to be a function of what one supposes
to represent a significant change. In short, our placement of
watersheds says more about the interests and questions with
which we interrogate the historical materials than about what
that history is supposedly speaking. For example, if one is
interested in the transition from "myth" to "philosophy" one
will perhaps look to classical Greece. If one prizes the tri-
umph of "reason" over "religious superstition" one will
probably find the Renaissance humanists of Northern Italy
and Paris candidates for a historical breakthrough. If the interests that move one are the revolution of "science" and
"the scientific attitude toward life" the Enlightenment is
likely to receive enthusiastic attention.

The questions we have been posing point us to a different
place — namely, to nineteenth-century Germany and the rise
of German historicism, together with the movement among
left-wing Hegelians represented by Feuerbach and Marx.
Marx will be the focus of our attention.[30]

Hegel made a famous comment on Kant's ethical imperative that one should never use another person as a means
but always as an end. "What," asked Hegel, "does that have
to do with the Norman conquest of England?" Hegel attempted to construct a meaning-system that would comprehend precisely such immoral (to Kant) but fundamentally
historical events as the conquest and subjugation of people
by war, the violent rise and fall of nations and civilizations,
the vitality and often viciousness of the world's history-
makers. Hegel was convinced that without such an attempt
one could not in fact "make sense" out of human historical
activity and would be reduced to writing marginal comments
on the personal ethics of a bedroom world.

In his *Philosophy of History*, Hegel set forth an embrac-
ing scheme of world history as the epiphany and self-
realization of the Universal Spirit or Absolute Idea. The
Universal Spirit "objectivates" itself — that is, projects itself
over against itself in becoming particular and embodied in

world-historical events and epochs. It thereby "alienates" itself as universal and ideal. The process of world history is the progress of this alienation of the Absolute Idea in the world, and its quest through history to "realize" and thereby return unto itself as universal. In short, Hegel viewed history as the dialectical process by which the Universal Spirit (or "God") comes to know and realize itself through the activity and consciousness of man.

History is thus valued — which Kant could not do — but not as *human* history. In the perspective of Hegel's historical idealism, man's history-making activity is not his own action. That is, it is not the history of himself in his own self-creation. Rather, man is projected as the function of some higher, transcendent activity. Consequently, man does not know himself as the product of his own historical productivity, but understands himself instead as being made (passively) by the activity of Another's self-making. In short, Hegel presents the consciousness of traditional man transposed, without essential change, into historical consciousness. It was Feuerbach who first grasped this criticism.

Man, Feuerbach argued, is not the alienation of the Universal Spirit, but the Universal Spirit is the alienation of man.[31] Hegel's Absolute Idea or "God" is the projection of man who has forgotten himself as the original projector. Robert Tucker has put it this way:

> Hegel's proposition that man is the revealed God is transformed into Feuerbach's proposition that God is the revealed man. The image of man as manifestation of divine substance gives way to the image of God as manifestation of human substance.[32]

Karl Marx drew upon this criticism of Hegel and gave perhaps its most succinct statement in stating: "the more of himself man attributes to God the less he has left in himself."[33] But Marx viewed Feuerbach as still too abstract and individual. "Feuerbach," Marx pointed out, resolves the essence of religion into the essence of man. But the essence of man is no abstraction inherent in each separate individual. In its reality it is the ensemble (aggregate) of social relations.[34]

In the process of developing his criticism of Feuerbach, Marx returned to Hegel and the latter's dialectical logic of history. Only now it is not the Universal Spirit which dialectically realizes itself through history; rather, it is man who creates himself through the dialectic of his collective activity in history. For Marx, man's actual relationship to himself is fundamentally human, active, and self-creative. His alienation, then, is not to know himself through his own activity but through the fiction of an activity of another — of God, or Nature, or Reason. Conversely, man's de-alienation results when Feuerbach's abstract criticism of heaven is turned into the concrete criticism of earth, the religious criticism into economic and social criticism. For, as Marx says, "not the gods nor nature but only man himself can be this alien power over man."[35]

In so saying, the early Marx turned not only Hegel but also Darwin "on his feet." Man is not a passive function of the self-evolution of Nature any more than he is that of God or of the Universal Spirit. Rather, nature becomes through human activity what it cannot become through itself. Man is not a natural animal but "a tool-making animal." He takes nature and transforms it in terms of his own human projects, and so transforms himself as a "natural, sensuous being."[36] In short, the early Marx's dialectical understanding of man set him against both idealism (Hegel) and naive materialism (Feuerbach). As such, it was the first clear statement of active man and of modern consciousness. The task of man's recovery is not obedience to Divine Authority, nor imitation of the rational-natural laws, nor a passive living-out of the self-evolution of the cosmos. It is, instead, his demystification of his human material and mental productions as *his own activity,* his active and conscious taking over of the human world as his own responsibility and risk. This, for Marx, was the actual condition of man, to become aware of which was to lose our "false consciousness" (Sartre's "bad faith"). It was the dialectical relationship of man to his given universe of reality.

Unfortunately, as the thought of Marx became transformed into Marxist orthodoxy, this active dialectical understanding of man was progressively lost. Now the dialectic *between man and his world* became a dialectic *within the economic-productive process* of which human consciousness is but an ancillary function and reflex. Man is no longer active in the fundamental sense of Marx's earlier dialectic. He has become a passive participant, knowing or otherwise, in the dialectical unfolding of the supra-human "laws" of the economic process, whose inevitable end, or realization, is the proletarian revolution. The only activity required of man is the passive activity of becoming aware, through the so-called scientific laws of history, of this opportunity and inevitability, and revolutionary conformity to what has thus been discovered.

But the science of history as finished accomplishment is precisely the loss of history as human activity. Man's activity becomes no longer his own, but a function and project of those very "scientific laws" he has himself projected and produced. The definer has become the defined. Marxism, it seems, falls into the trap which Marx originally set for others. It loses grasp of man's production of explanations as man's own activity and so falls victim to an abstract explanation fetishism. That is, it fails to notice the on-going project of the explainer hidden behind the finished form of the explanation. But in fact explanation is the midwife of man's unfinished project of consciousness. It transforms man's activity in the world into conscious activity, changing the relationship of man to that explained from an undialectical and organic to a transcending and innovative relationship. Consequently, an

explanation which understands itself as final and complete
has lost grasp of itself as human project and activity. It does
not notice that it is already behind man's activity in the
world because man's consciousness is already driving ahead
with its transformed project on the basis which it, as explanation, has just laid.

This fetish of explanation left orthodox Marxists at a
complete loss to explain how the twentieth century could
(and must!) have happened the way it did. Viewing the
world through their authoritative and finished explanation
— that is, a dialectical interpretation that has, without noticing it, lost its dialectic — they could not reach man in his concrete historical activity; they reached only a forced abstraction as refracted through their own prior-defining activity.
Marxism, in short, *forgot itself*. It forgot that its own dialectical analysis of the "laws" of economic process was itself a
human, ideational product whose validity could be altered
by subsequent human activity either not anticipated in the
original explanation or perhaps set loose by it to move beyond
it. To be sure, this reduction of human history to the laws
of economic process carried the practical benefit of securing
to the suppressed proletariat the "guarantee" of history. Indeed, this hope proved essential in awakening the narcotized
worker to his revolutionary destiny. But precisely this fact
points to the deeper reason for Marxism's self-forgetful re-
treat into explanation fetishism — namely, its inadequate
understanding of human "needs." This failure can be traced
back to Marx himself.

Marx tended to reduce the essential needs of man to
"physical, sensuous needs." In so doing, he failed to see
that man has a need for meaning — a unifying perspective of
interpretation and hope — of which his own project of a
classless and humane society became a prime historical example. As fundamental as his need for food, shelter, sex, and
other basic requirements, is man's need to create a universe
of meaning and value, to define his situation as significant, to

make of this place where he finds himself an understandable and familiar place. The latter need arises as a necessity and inevitability for man precisely as a conscious being, as *a need of consciousness*. In turn, these idea systems (the superstructure) interact with — that is, are something more than a passive reflection of — the system of economic production (the substructure). The two levels of human creation — ideational and material — reciprocally influence and act back, one upon the other.

It was Max Weber who developed this point in his brilliant sociological studies of religion and of religious ideas. Weber stated this position in his *Sociology of Religion* in connection with the particular religious development that interested him. "The need for salvation and ethical religion," he pointed out,

> has yet another source besides the social condition of the disprivileged and the rationalism of the middle classes, which are projects of their practical way of life. This additional factor is intellectualism as such, more particularly the metaphysical needs of the human mind as it is driven to reflect on ethical and religious questions, driven not by material need but by an inner compulsion to understand the world as a meaningful cosmos and to take up a position toward it.[37]

This insight into man as a meaning-needing and meaning-producing being stabilizes the pole of consciousness in its dialectical interaction with the given form of the material world, returning to the fully active view of man in the early Marx. Weber, of course, was no idealist. Man's drive for "making sense out of his life" is man's own drive and sense-making, and, as such, relative to the actual conditions of his everyday activity in the world. That is, ideas cannot simply pop into being; they arise out of the interaction of man's consciousness and the given form of his mundane life. On the other hand, consciousness and its productions are not simply an epiphenomenal reflex; significance-systems have a certain logic and inner life of their own, as well as the weight to act back upon the material conditions of the world and change them, even as they are changed by those conditions. Indeed, it is only on this basis that one can begin to interpret why eastern and western civilizations should have developed so differently, one from the other.

The importance of this corrective stabilization of consciousness in its relationship to the world can be illustrated by a few examples of the struggle of man today to surpass the explanation fetishisms that dehumanize him as surely as his commodity fetishism does, thus making him a stranger (a passive passenger) in his own world. These examples will also serve as a fit summary to the overall thesis here: that the fundamental reality of modern man is his revolution from a passive to an active consciousness. Man's perception of himself has become that of a being who must constantly overcome and transcend himself in order to remain "his own" in a human world.

THE UNFINISHED REVOLUTION OF
ACTIVE CONSCIOUSNESS

"Sex is natural." This seems to be the socially most general *idea* by means of which modern western societies seek to explain man's sexuality and define his situation in this regard. It is also, as we shall see, a lively source of contemporary explanation fetishism. To tell oneself that sex is "natural" is to know one's sexuality not as human and humanly defined, but as a product and definition of another source — in this case, of "nature." But in fact nature has in this respect no stable connotations except the connotations which man originally gives it. It is a *human* word and definition; so that what man hears when he hears this word is in fact his own prior-defining activity. Insofar as he forgets this, man does not know his sexuality as his own human activity, but passively receives and defines himself in terms of his alienated mental productions. The process of sexual de-alienation is therefore the disenchantment of "nature" by rediscovering it as man's own defining activity.

Sigmund Freud seems central in this historical task of rediscovering just how nature came to mean what it does in this regard. Yet behind Freud lies a tradition going back to the Enlightenment and the image of the mathematico/ geometric world-machine that was extrapolated from the (historically contingent) rise of modern science out of seventeenth-century astronomy. Freud added to this inherited model of nature the images of "instinct" and "satisfaction" — of "tension," "release," and return to "statis" — which he imported from the science of water that was developing during the latter half of the nineteenth century. This was the "idea" by which he then explained the dynamics of human sexual behavior. To be sure, Freud did not know this mechanical/impulse-release model of nature as his own human project and defining activity. Rather, he understood man — and especially sexual man — as defined (passively) by this "nature" whose definition he, Freud, had in fact produced.

The result of the subsequent massive social surrender to this explanation fetishism is all too evident today. We are familiar, for example, with the dehumanizing consequences of the frantic search to know ourselves as "natural" — that is, sexually normal — through the perfection of the mechanics of impulse and release, through the cosmic blessing of mutual orgasm. We are familiar with this alien third projected between two people in the most intimate of *human* relations — this "performance standard" to which we offer the worship of our hope for success and of our dread of inadequacy. We hear the persistent voices of the priests of this explanation fetishism — men who make money from the loss of our activity as human activity — whether the scriptures they write be *Playboy* "competence" or marriage manual "how to. . . ."

In short, we are well acquainted with this loss of our defining activity as in fact our own, when we relate sexually to one another not as persons but as two "natures" caught in the cosmic necessity of "instinct," "drive," and "satisfaction," of pneumatic anxiety seeking pneumatic perfection. We are "not our own" but nature's. The definer has become the defined.

The project of regaining a grasp on our lives as *human in a human world* is the disenchantment of this explanation fetishism. It is, quite precisely, the reassertion of *our right to be human with one another* instead of "natural." Thus man's task of de-alienation is not merely material but also mental. The producer must regain control over *all* his products. The fact that this is presently happening — for example, in the movie *The Graduate* and what it represents more broadly in the passage of the younger generation beyond the taboos and reverse taboos of its elders — supports the contention that modern man is in fact moving from a passive to an active consciousness; that is, to a dialectical understanding of himself in relation to the sociohistorical production of the given universe of reality. That this remains an "unfinished revolution" also seems evident.

A second example of our general thesis may be found in the traditional "ideas" which serve to explain and define the situation of American industrial society. Karl Marx has warned us that

> Insofar as [the ruling individuals] rule as a class and determine the extent and compass of an epoch, it is self-evident that they do this in their whole range, hence among other things [they] rule also as thinkers and producers of ideas, and regulate the production and distribution of the ideas of their age: thus their ideas are the ruling ideas of the epoch.[38]

"Upward mobility" and "middle-class affluent society"

seem the two most important contemporary societal explana-
tion-ideas. An examination of them will indicate whether
Marx's anticipation of a fetishism of explanation is correct in
regard to them.

The undeniably conservative function of these two intellectual productions, their role in legitimating and maintain-
ing the rules of the given social game, should be noted at the
start. The ideas of upward mobility and middle-class affluent
society tranquilize radical social protest, confining the dynamics of sub-group pressure within the approved definition
of social reality. To the lower stratifications of society these
explanation-images proclaim present possession of material
prosperity, together with promise of further accumulation
as the reward of playing the social contest by the established
rules. It is illuminating in this regard to examine the idea of
upward mobility in detail. There is, if this image is accurate,
sharp movement among various social strata, sub-groups making jumps upward relative to their prior social location. Yet,
to examine closely the implied connotation is to reveal the
hidden fetishism of this explanation. For in fact groups
within the American social process have remained fairly
static in the percentage, so to speak, of prestige and material
reward allocated to them in the overall social marketplace.[39]
What has happened is a rapid expansion of the productive
system as a whole; various sub-groups receive bigger pieces
of pie only because the pie itself has grown rapidly larger,
the percentage distribution remaining relatively stable. Not
upward mobility but growth of the gross national product
has been the way in which American society has kept the
lid on lower-strata pressures for "advancement."

It is here that the social function of the idea of "middle-
class affluent society" becomes evident. It is a narcotizing image which deflects attention from the massive wealth ac-
cumulated by special groups and sectors within the total
social marketplace.[40] A brief analytical look at the structure

of this fabled mass affluence will uncover its reality as alienation and false consciousness.

The *New York Times* of November 18, 1968 reported
the following set of income statistics for that year. From
them, a startling picture emerges. The figures, let it be noted,
cover only *white families*. The largest income group (25.1 per
cent of the total white population) received $7,000 to $9,999
per year. But in order to achieve this level, 56.1 per cent of
these families had to have "two or more wage earners." The
next largest group (22.5 per cent of all white families)
earned "under $5,000" per year. In order to achieve an annual
income of $10,000 to $11,999, 66.9 per cent of the families
in that bracket had to have two or more wage earners. Of
those families with incomes of $12,000 to $14,999 per year,
75.9 per cent attained that level only with two or more
wage earners. These statistics could be elaborated further,
but the actual picture is already clear. Almost 50 per cent of
the *white families* in America live either far below or just at the
$9,000-plus level projected by the government at that time
as necessary for a moderate middle-class style of life in urban
communities. And of this percentage, more than half the
families had to depend upon two wage earners to achieve
even this minimal middle-class status. In short, there is not
massive "affluence" but massive moonlighting. If one adds
to these statistics the figures from the black community, the
actual situation of American society becomes even clearer:
we are in fact neither "upwardly mobile" (in any real sense)
nor "middle-class and affluent." We are instead sleepwalking
within a social explanation that deflects us from noticing our
actual situation, that defuses social anger, and maintains the
given game and rules of society — a brokering system, it might
be noted, from which a small minority derives great and continuing wealth. Marx's prediction of a fetishism of explanation, it would seem, is borne out by the statistics.

It is precisely these actualities of the American social
system that the New Left is bringing insistently to our atten-

tion. American society, it points out, remains essentially what it has always been: inordinately unequal, although denying it. New Left members call attention to this despite cries from the keepers of the given universe of reality of "anarchism," "communism," and "bad child psychology." Once again, in short, there are signs of man's movement from a passive to an active consciousness, of his de-alienating struggle to regrasp the realities of his life from those mental productions of which he has become a product himself. Here too, of course, the revolution in consciousness remains partial and undeveloped. The potential new majority coalition resists recognizing itself; interpretive lines continue to be drawn through American society where they do not belong — for example, between two such mutually exploited groups as students and police, or between most blue/white-collar workers and the poor on welfare. Yet a restless sense that something is being "put over on us" remains among the vast majority, which waits to discover its own reality out of the self-forgetfulness induced by the traditional images of American social explanation.

A third example, and a fit conclusion to this general thesis, is to be found in modern man's passage from a passive to an active consciousness concerning the nurture and preservation of his *homeland earth*. Curiously, what is probably the most consequential effect of the space program was completely unanticipated by its technical planners, namely, that man should begin to see himself as seen, and to interpret himself as interpreted in the picture of the earthrise over the moonscape. For the first time man begins now to know himself as a member and citizen not of some parochial place and history within the world but *of the world itself* — man's bright blue agate — and of the human experiment which is tied so inexorably to it. As a result, this is the first generation in human history for which the primary question of existence becomes not "how shall we make it in the world?" but "can the world make it?" Indeed, it is precisely this *new worldliness* (in a profound sense), this worldly seriousness, that marks one of the most fundamental aspects of the generation gap.

For many of the younger generation see the issue confronting their lives as not, first of all, the discovery of some parochial enclave of success and security within the workaday world. Rather, they begin to know themselves as those in whose life-activity the answer will be found, in one way or another, to the question of whether the world will work. Here is a basic shift in the perception of self-interest which the older generation of world-definers (political, social, and theological realists of various stamp) have not been able to grasp at all, or which they have misinterpreted as a new naiveté or a utopianism. That is why the definitions of reality of a Dean Rusk or a Richard Nixon appear so parochial and inadequate to many of the younger generation, for whom the essential issue is not the obvious givenness of the nation-state and its precarious adjudication of competing national interests, but the nurture and preservation of a world in which man may survive the consequences of his own activity. At a deeper level, what is happening here is a fundamental emigration of man from a passive consciousness which takes the world for granted, and so preoccupies itself with enclaves of hope, value, and success within the world, to man's active perception of himself as one who most literally *has the world on his hands.*

This is the new and radically transformed worldliness, realism, and perception of self-interest that moves and disturbs so many of the students today. It is the sense that, willy-nilly, man does participate in creating (or destroying) his own future, and has therefore not simply the right but the absolute necessity of realizing this reality in a changed social structure and practice. It is the sense that there will be no forgiveness for man's continuing trespass of his global home, but only the forlorn silence of just another solar system which, for a while, was magnificently adorned with the voices from a bright blue agate. In short, the revolution in consciousness of modern man goes far deeper in its roots and requirements than disenchantment with the war policy of a particular government or the administration of a particular university or even the degradation of a racial minority in a particular society. These are but the visible portions (what we can get our hands on) of an iceberg whose depths reach into man's most basic perception of the way he is in the world, and of his life-situation and its definition in this regard.

To this extent it does not seem outrageously naive to speak about a "new man" or a "new humanity." In fact, it seems the most truly realistic way to speak, since it is reality and man's perception and construction of it that are involved. At the heart of this lies a new consciousness, a revolution in the way man understands himself in the world. He comes to know himself now as an active citizen and caretaker of this homeland earth who must bear, without benefit of external intervention, the consequences of his own world-making and world-shattering activity. Life-explanations that do not take this radically transformed human self-perception into account will increasingly be seen not only as inadequate but in fact dangerous to man. This means that active man is beginning to know that, for all its attractive securities, he cannot much longer afford the traditional consciousness of passive man, that without this "coming of age" there is little likelihood of a human age to come. And in this, he is truly a "new man," one not before known in the history of human self-interpretation, a man aware that he can no longer afford to know himself as "not his own."

NOTES

1. Mircea Eliade, *Cosmos and History* (New York: Harper, 1959), p. 156.

2. This is not to deny that modern man also lives passively, in terms of his socialization into a common universe of discourse (e.g., language) and into a shared and largely taken-for-granted set of predictions and anticipations that comprise and make possible a social "world." But modern man knows this passivity of socialization and knows himself in the midst of it. That is, he has named and studied it as his own social activity and creation. He is no longer in an uncritical relationship to the social universe of which he is a part. Consequently, in terms of his consciousness, the passivity of socialization becomes an enclave within the wider, active consciousness of man who knows himself as the producer of all socializations and, as such, the producer of himself.

3. Eric Voegelin, *Israel and Revelation* (Baton Rouge: Louisiana State University Press, 1948), p. 3.

4. Henri Frankfort, *Kingship and the Gods* (Chicago: University of Chicago Press, 1948), p. 3.

5. For documentation, see Hannah Arendt, *The Human Condition;* also, Ernst Cassirer, *The Myth of the State.*

6. *Republic*, trans. F. M. Cornford (Oxford: Clarendon Press, 1941), 501 a/b.

7. Eliade, *op. cit.*, p. 123.

8. See Ernst Troeltsch, *The Social Teaching of the Christian Churches* (New York: Macmillan, 1956), vol. 1; and A. H. Armstrong, *The Architecture of the Intelligible Universe.* Troeltsch shows the influence of stoic rationalism and legal theory on the construction of the primitive Christian ethic. Armstrong analyzes the neoplatonic cosmology which so affected the patristic apologists.

9. It did have the ethical resources of Rabbinic Judaism which already reflected the impact of the intellectuality of classical Greek idealism. But the primitive Christian communities did not feel the need to develop these notions systematically until it became evident that the parousia was to be delayed. Only then did the Christian's "situation in the world" require fuller and theoretically more serious explication. For the most part this development is to be found outside the canonical scriptures in the apologetic and theological productions of the patristic period. John Noonan in his book, *Contraception*, is aware of the stoic influence on early Christian sex ethic; but he does not develop this theme as we do here.

10. *City of God*, xix, 13 (all quotations taken from the Modern Library edition).

11. *City of God*, xii, 5, emphasis added.

12. Troeltsch, *op. cit.*, vol. 1, pp. 201–256.

13. James Bryce, Viscount, *The Holy Roman Empire* (New York: The Macmillan Co., 1871), p. 96.

14. Quoted from R. W. and A. J. Carlyle, *History of Mediaeval Political Theory* (London: Blackwood and Sons, 1956), vol. 4, p. 166.

15. Quoted from Troeltsch, *op. cit.*, vol. 1, p. 386, n. 89.

16. Adolf von Gierke, *Political Theories of the Middle Ages*, trans. F. W. Maitland (Cambridge, England: University Press, 1900), p. 10.

17. Michael Wilk's book, *The Problem of Sovereignty in the Later Middle Ages* (Cambridge, England: University Press, 1964), is especially illuminating on this subject.

18. Troeltsch, *op. cit.* pp. 256–327.

19. Compare *City of God*, xi, 21.

20. This is Thomas' doctrine of subsidiarity; see *S.T.* I-II, qq. 94 and 109; II-II, q. 10; I-III a. iv, 1; also *De Reg. Princ.* I, 1 and *Comm. in Nich. Eth.* I, 1.

21. *S.T.* I-II, q. 97, emphasis added.

22. Leslie Dewart in *The Future of Belief* poses the same question we do here and comes to the same conclusions. Some of the subsequent criticisms of that book seem to arise from a misunderstanding of the questions Dewart is asking — namely, his full familiarity with the Marxist concepts of "alienation" and "reification."

23. *Institutes*, I, 2, 8 (Library of Christian Classics edition).

24. Quoted from François Wendel, *John Calvin*, trans. Philip Mairet (New York: Harper and Rowe, 1963), p. 38.

25. See *Inst.* II, 2, 7.

26. Max Weber in *The Protestant Ethic and the Spirit of Capitalism* formulated the "vessel" and "tool" concepts as ideal types of religious self-understanding.

27. Commentary on Genesis 1:26 in *Calvin's Commentaries*, ed. J. Haroutunian (Philadelphia: Westminster Press, 1958), p. 357, emphasis added.

28. *Inst.* II, 7, 1.

29. A complete treatment of this transformation would have to include an economic, political, and social/institutional history. Here we treat only the "ideational" pole of the dialectic. But ideas, as we have seen, do not develop as a pure dialectic of ideas. Thus, the development of an increasingly refined division of labor, the rise of money economy, specialization of various sub-processes and sub-societies within the overall social world, increasing secularization through religious pluralism and contact with the industrial/technological form of labor — all these events in the material/institutional world played a central role in the dialectic of the developing ideational system.

30. Van Harvey's book, *The Historian and the Believer*, is an account of the problem of historicism and the issues it raises for traditional Christian thought.

31. Feuerbach develops this idea in his *Essence of Christianity*.

32. *Philosophy and Myth in Karl Marx* (Cambridge, England: University Press, 1961), p. 83.

33. Marx, *Economic and Philosophical Manuscripts*, from *Marx's Concept of Man*, ed. Erich Fromm, trans T. Bottomore (New York: Frederick Ungar, 1961), p. 96.

34. *Ibid.* p. 78.

35. *Ibid.* p. 104.

36. See Louis Dupré, *The Philosophical Foundations of Marxism* (New York: Harcourt, Brace and World, 1966); especially where Dupré develops Marx's criticism of Feuerbach.

37. Max Weber, *Sociology of Religion*, ed. Talcott Parsons (Boston: Beacon Press, 1964), p. 148.

38. Quoted from Dupré, *Philosophical Foundations of Marxism*, p. 157.

39. E. Digby Balzell's *The Protestant Establishment* offers an interesting analysis and documentation of this point.

40. See C. Wright Mills, *The Power Elite* (New York: Oxford University Press, 1959).

THE SITUATION OF CHRISTIAN RADICALS

Paul M. van Buren

However we may feel about the desirability and the possibility of revolution (cultural or political or both), it is clear that there exists a widespread sense of moral outrage and aesthetic disgust concerning important aspects of the present form of life of western culture. The outrage and disgust are to be seen above all in the incipient revolt of the student generation, from Berkeley to Berlin, against an oppressive, sick society; they are evident as well in the writings of Herbert Marcuse. The same sentiments may also be found in those taking part in all sorts of underground and so-called radical religious movements. Professor Marcuse has suggested that religious radicals are allied with all who work for human liberation, just as he implies that the churches are allied with all the other forms of oppressive establishment. Leaving to one side the question of the churches, I wish in this essay to consider the ambiguous situation of those "religious radicals" in our society who, in one way or another, have for reasons of conscience turned away from the churches. The ambiguity of their situation is suggested by the word which Marcuse has used — heretical — and is to be found in the fact that their relation to their own religious traditions is that, not of "affiliation," or "preference," but of partial alienation: their religious identity is best discovered by asking what church they stay away from. The number of such ex- or quasi- or on-or-just-beyond-the-fringe Christians, who find themselves sharing the widespread outrage and disgust concerning a society seen as oppressive and diseased, is sufficiently large (and apparently growing), and their position sufficiently ambiguous, to warrant examination as one aspect of the present situation. In any case, theirs is the situation that will be explored in this essay.

Religious radicalism, however, is itself too ambiguous a term to indicate the subject, for it may refer to a position of political radicalism when held by people of fairly traditional religious convictions, or it could refer to radical reinterpretations of religion by persons uninvolved in radical politics. Political radicalism and theological radicalism are not, after all, necessarily allied. Outrage at the oppressive, inhuman character of the military-industrial-educational-ecclesiastical complex can be and is found among people who have not rebelled against the system of thought which traditional Christianity has produced. There are those, however, who conjoin moral outrage in the face of the military-industrial-educational-ecclesiastical establishment of our society with a search for what some have called a radical new interpretation of Christianity. It is the situation of such persons that concerns us here.

The ambiguity of their situation lies not simply in their alienation from the churches. It lies also in their very pursuit of a radical Christianity. To put it simply, can they be both radical and Christian at the same time? Whether we call their position secular Christianity, non-religious faith, or radical religion, is there not an inevitable contradiction in terms in the very project? If we are really at the end of the road, to use

Professor Shaull's figure, can there be a new beginning for Christianity? Is not the situation we are investigating really that of certain people who are simply on their way out of Christianity altogether, people who perhaps need only a bit of therapy, philosophical or psychological in nature, to free them from the hold of their past? Or can some sense be made of their conviction that they are on the way to a new religious position, one which both responds to and enriches contemporary sensibility just as much as an older religion responded to and enriched an older sensibility?

These questions are fraught with problems and puzzles. In attempting to arrive at a reasonably fair answer, one cannot hope to deal with all that should be taken into consideration. Two sets of "lines of force," as it were, radiate from the two poles of political and theological radicalism, and they crisscross each other at many points. One can't pretend to map all these points but it may be that by looking with care at one crossing point, we shall be a step closer to understanding the larger picture. If one piece of the picture could become clearer, it might help to see other parts better.

It should be obvious, then, that I do not pretend here to speak of, much less speak for, all those who have been influenced by the sensibility or self-understanding which in varying degrees marks the present temper of revolt and protest, and who at the same time find themselves in a relationship to the Christian tradition ranging from full acceptance to painful alienation. What is intended here is as clear a definition as possible of one actual position, in the light of which other positions relatively nearby may be better understood.

The position to be defined can be made clear by exploring the answers to a number of questions which can be raised. We can ask about the past and present relationship of these Christian radicals to the Christian tradition. It is an important aspect of their present situation that they once identified themselves as men in the world by reference to this tradition. But we shall also have to ask about their relationship to contemporary consciousness, for their growing affirmative or, at the very least, participatory role within this consciousness has led them to break in important ways with the Christian tradition. By exploring the character of this consciousness (or those aspects of it which have caused them to change their relationship to Christianity), the reasons why they have reached their present point, and why they continue to maintain a relationship with the Christian tradition at all may be clarified.

RADICAL CHRISTIANS AND THE CHRISTIAN TRADITION

First, let us consider where our selected group of radical Christians stand with respect to the Christian tradition. In most cases they are in a situation of partial alienation. That is to say, there was a time for most of them in which they regarded that tradition, or more accurately, one or another of the varieties of that tradition, as their own. The variety of traditions which have gone to make up what is called Christianity need not concern us here. That variety was the concern of the ecumenical movement, but the ecumenical issue of the unification of those various traditions, inevitably to be worked out in an ecclesiastical framework, has long since ceased to be of interest to those alienated from one or another of those churches, people whose questions about any and all those traditions are the same. What has changed for radical Christians is their relationship to precisely those fundamentals on which all the churches could agree. What made the ecumenical movement possible is itself what is now being questioned, or at least seen in a new light. Christianity was once viewed as the institution which provided the answer to life's great questions; God was that to which all things finally related; and faith in God, or in God-in-Christ, gave a final orientation to life. Variations in the interpretation of the Christian story, or message, or tradition, or life, or affirmation (whichever combination of these may have been involved in any particular case) may once have seemed important. For the radical Christian, however, it is more important that it was once true, but is no longer so, that he heard that story as his own story, that that message was the message above all else he heard, that that was the affirmation he wanted and was able to make.

In one way or another, it has happened to our radical Christian, as to many others, that he has found himself unable to go on saying what he had been saying. It has come to bother him more and more that the churches keep insisting that the story is a true story. It has come to seem less and less tenable to hold that the message covers all of life. Increasingly he has found that if the affirmations of religion are held to involve making claims, then he wants out. Perhaps that is not quite it. Perhaps it would be better to say that he has come to think that affirmations are of many sorts, that religion has no monopoly on them, and in fact no longer gives him the words he wants for making some of his most important affirmations. He wants to affirm life, not the church; to affirm man and not God; to confess the utter mess we are making of the human experiment, not a doctrine of sin. How many are there who learned from the church the meaning of celebration, and have come to the point at which they now find themselves, longing to celebrate something, but certainly not able to do that in the churches, indeed no longer sure that the churches want to celebrate what they want to celebrate!

Where are they, then, with respect to Christianity? The people I have in mind are surely not among those who don't give Christianity a thought and couldn't care less about the Christian story. This was their story, and now it remains for them a story that matters, but not the one and only story that needs telling. This was their tradition, but now it has become only one of the traditions that make up their past as they now see it. These were affirmations they once made, but which they can neither make nor deny, for to deny them seems as silly, as aside the point, somehow, as affirming them. They are in a definite relationship to the part of their past broadly defined as Christianity, but the relationship is one of partial alienation. They are alienated from those who defend the tradition against contemporary sensibility by insisting that Christianity today must be what it is claimed always to have been. To say these people are alienated from the tradition says too much. For them the tradition is not so much wrong as inadequate to their present experience. It says both too much and too little, for reasons that will be clarified. This is what is meant by partial alienation.

THE SHIFT IN CONTEMPORARY SELF-CONSCIOUSNESS

Such alienation has not just happened. Most who are in this situation would probably admit in some way that this has happened because they have come to hear other stories, other messages, because they have come to share in another self-understanding than that provided by the Christian tradition. In order to comprehend their situation, then, we must look to the self-consciousness of our times. It is necessary to do so because there are important differences of emphasis or valuation between contemporary culture and that older culture (or cultures, preferably, for in this area, the Hellenistic, Roman, and Medieval cultures stand as one in contrast to that of the present era) in which Christianity grew up, from which it drew so much, and to which it made its own contribution. In that process Christianity came to be, or was already in its very beginnings, part and parcel of a way of thinking, a way of putting the world together, a way of asking questions as well as of answering them, which is surely still with us in some degree, but which no longer dominates the self-understanding of many men or their comprehension of their place in the universe. In short, a cultural shift has been taking place (and still is), a shift which lies behind, or which may be read from, a good deal of contemporary radicalism, whether that radicalism is cultural, political, or religious in nature.

This shift is doubtless what is being referred to when people speak of secularism and of secularization. These terms are singularly unilluminating, although they once seemed to offer a clue to what has happened to us. The terms are so conditioned by their fundamentally theological or religious character (who but a theologian would think today of calling banking a "secular" occupation?) that they are both misleading words to use for descriptive purposes, and increasingly inappropriate for men whose relationship to Christianity is that of partial but serious alienation. We should instead turn our attention to the shift that appears to be under way: a tendency in our contemporary self-understanding and value structure which seems to place us in a world different from that in which the Christian tradition was more or less at home. I would single out as distinguishing features of this shift a different attitude toward change, toward particulars, toward plurality and relativity, and a new sense of ourselves as the active agents who make our own future. Let me enlarge briefly on these five features. In doing so I shall try to draw out the ambiguities of this shift which show up in the radical movement of our time.

The first, if not necessarily the most important, feature of the cultural shift that has placed the radical Christian where he is now is the tendency so evident in innumerable areas of life to regard change, flexibility, and fluidity as a norm or a positive good. The most casual acquaintance with the political, economic, philosophical, or religious literature of the past makes us aware how deeply men used to dread change, how men longed for the security of permanence. As we come to see this, we become aware that we have come to take change for granted and to admire what is flexible, open to innovation, adjustment, and reconstruction — not settled for all time or immovably fixed. As we view the matter now, it is possible to say that things have always been in change, that every age was an age of transition; but today we are aware, perhaps because of the geometrically increasing rate of change, that "the name of the game is change." We do not resent this, as our grandfathers would have done. Uneven and incomplete as is this shift of attitude toward change, the fact that it exists to the extent that it does marks us off from men in most of recorded history.

The effects on our age of this shift are various, not only because each of us responds to it in various degrees, but also because it produces attitudes by no means mutually congenial. For some it has meant a release from dogmatism, an openness to the novel, a willingness to experiment in all areas of human life. For others, however, it has produced a sense of living in the moment, a willingness to shift with each change of fashion, to take up each new fad, to surrender oneself to immediate satisfaction without regard to past or future. It is perhaps important to those of radical persuasion that they understand that precisely those shifts in human consciousness which have made their own position possible have at the same time created the very situations and conditions against which they revolt. The disgust they feel toward the inhuman consumer society of our day is brought into focus by two incompatible movements of a single cultural shift. Acceptance of change may mark us all today, but it is an ambiguous marking.

Not unrelated to a new appreciation of change is an increasing concern with particulars. "Humanity," not to speak of "human nature," seems to us an abstraction, less high on our "reality scale" than are specific people. In our own way, we are more nominalistic than our forefathers, more convinced that each thing is itself, each person himself, and that such particularity ought to be respected. Empiricism may account for part of this newer valuation of particulars; undoubtedly the scientific method and its results have been crucial in bringing about our present view of ourselves and our world.

This aspect or tendency of the cultural shift that separates us to some degree from the past is as ambiguous as our changed attitude toward change. It can work to produce a distrust of the large generalizations and abstractions by which the establishment seeks to turn our eyes away from the particulars of its policies and practices in matters of race and war, but the same tendency can lead to a somnolent uninvolvement, a contented submersion in the multitude of things produced by a consumer-oriented economy. It's not only the members of the SDS, the New Left, or the Black Panthers who each "do their own thing"; so do the suburban consumers and the vast numbers of unreflective aficionados of the idiot box.

This same ambiguity shows up if the cultural shift through which we are passing is viewed as a movement toward pluralism. The world of our experience is a world in so many different ways that any of the unities discovered in things are always unities for some particular purpose, unities that leave room for other ways in which the world is also a world for us. The plurality of our experience, in short, as it comes to be recognized and acknowledged, leads to a pluralism in our thinking and understanding.

Pluralism, as distinguished from any form of monistic understanding of things (whether monism of a naturalistic or a theistic sort) can lead to flexibility in thought and action. It can open one to empathetic appreciation of other peoples and races, to the desire to allow each to make his special contribution. It can provide a healthy check on latent tendencies to dogmatism and fanaticism. It closes the door on the dangers of absolutism. In this way, it can open for us the possibility of working for creative new steps ahead in the human enterprise without becoming blocked by the fact that we have no perfect image, no absolute goal, no final answers to anything. It frees us to feel that it is good and right to explore, to invent, to experiment, even to talk of "revolution for the hell of it."

This same pluralism, however, can produce that state of unreflective immediacy so characteristic of many in our time. Pluralism doesn't force one to creativity. If it opens that possibility, if room is made for the genuinely novel, then room

is also made for that nonchalant justification of avoidance of
all possible choices, of evasion of conflict and decision. Many
people in our society reveal the pluralism of their thinking
by viewing all things as possibilities, none as necessities; therefore there seems no reason for doing anything about anything, except in the small private world such people make for
themselves.

The other side of the coin called pluralism is relativism.
The times are marked by an increasing sense of the relativity
of things. What is true for us is increasingly conceived as
being true always and only relative to some specifiable frame
of reference. Absolutes come to be increasingly distrusted;
"dogmatic" becomes a word increasingly difficult to disasso-
ciate from pejorative connotations.

The negative effects of relativism have been pointed out
frequently enough to need little elaboration. In sum, relativism can lead to apathy, to unreflective immediacy, to uninvolvement in the conflicts and issues dividing society. Since
all things are relative, why bother, why get involved? What
is true for you is your business, not mine. This response to
relativism is easy enough to see today. But relativism as a
feature of a tendency in our thinking is also producing contrary effects. At the level of reflection, it leads us to wrestle
with a new awareness of our immediate involvement with all
we speak of, to the extent that we begin to see that all we
speak of is what it is for us in and with our speaking of it.
Existentialists, Phenomenologists, and Analysts have expressed
this in differing ways, but there is also a deeper commonality
in these different philosophical movements. Once we begin
to see our world as ours, as the world we not only find but
which we also shape by our ways of apprehending it, once
we see that knowledge is always our knowledge, that science
is our human science, then the world becomes humanized
for us. Our gods are our own, as we are our own; and now,
as the fruit of a full-blown relativism, there arises the possibility for responsibility, for commitment, for action, since we

know full well, not without a tinge of irony, that the future of our world lies, for better or worse, in our own hands. To put the matter in other terms, once we have become aware of the sociology of knowledge, we can either give up talking about knowledge at all, or, with a touch of irony, we can persist in speaking of what we "know," in the realization that tomorrow depends on which shade of gray we work for, perhaps even die for.

John Raines, in his essay in this volume, has put the matter in another way by speaking of a shift in human self-consciousness: we are coming to see ourselves as active agents of our lives, rather than as passive creatures of an order that is "given," whether by a god, an inexorable "Nature," fate, or anything else. It would be easy to attack an oversimplification of Raines' thesis and thereby miss this important feature of what I have been calling a cultural shift. Never before in human history, it could be said, have men been more sensitive to the ways in which they have been conditioned by their economic, social, and political environment, or by psychological forces and racial attitudes. Yet the very fact of this sensitivity reflects a conviction that these factors could have been changed, and that they can be changed for the future. Things don't have to go on being the same way, we seem to feel. If we go on polluting the earth, continuing to follow dehumanizing racial patterns, and accepting oppressive economic structures, it will be our own fault.

I am not arguing that we shall in fact be able to change these conditions of human life. Whether we succeed or fail, however, the fact remains that we are coming to think of ourselves as the active creators of our own future. The human experiment, we are beginning to feel, rests in our own fallible hands. The ambiguity of response to this new dimension of human self-consciousness is self-evident.

These elements of contemporary self-awareness have been sketched because it has been the impact of this cultural shift that has contributed so largely to the inability of many Christians to remain attached to their religion as they once were. The ambiguous character of these elements has also been mentioned because it is the problem posed by these ambiguities which accounts for the radical Christians' present position. Let us look at these in order.

THE CONTEMPORARY SITUATION OF CHRISTIAN RADICALS

There can be nothing surprising in the fact that the impact upon Christians of the cultural shift which marks off the modern period (and especially the past hundred years) from the period in which Christianity began and took shape, has been to loosen the hold of their faith over them. The response to contemporary consciousness has taken a variety of forms, from attempting to isolate faith from the demands of contemporary consciousness, through partial accommodations of the faith to the times, to total rejection of a faith no longer able to survive in the newer climate. The crisis of faith through which so many are passing now is in many ways only another stage of the crisis that has been with us for over a century. New only is the fact that increasingly the key issue, the doctrine of God, or the problem of theism, is no longer an issue for our culture, because, due to past stages of this crisis, the question about God has become almost totally peripheral to the major concerns of our time.[1]

To put the matter starkly, the classical doctrine of God runs into tremendous difficulties when set in the context of modern science and modern philosophy. It could survive in one way or another if it had to contend with the scientific method only, for we all know able scientists who manage this. It can also survive rigorous critical thought, so long as the impact of the scientific revolution is ignored. But when the scientific and philosophical revolutions of modern times together win their place as the foundation for thought, then traditional theism has difficulties so great as to be increasingly untenable for educated persons.[2]

We are aware by now that there seems to be no end of possible arguments thought up to show that while the difficulties are great, they are not insuperable. A great deal of time will have to be expended trying to show that the difficulties remain in spite of the new arguments. This means that, instead of acknowledging that theism won't do any longer, and getting on to constructive thinking about the options that remain, a lot of time will have to be wasted cleaning up the ground over which history has washed in the past few centuries. Since, for the purposes of this essay, I wish to see where the radicals may be heading, I shall simply have to confess that many arguments for theism have not been exhaustively refuted, that that argument will still go on, and that by turning my back on it, I have not settled the matter to the satisfaction of those who wish to continue to defend theism.

For many Christians, however, it is becoming increasingly clear that they do not believe there is a God who acts in the world at the present time, who ever acted in the world in the past, or who will act in the world in the future in any way corresponding to the manner in which we think of any agent acting in the world. Nor do they believe that there is someone "there," on the other end of the line, so to speak, to whom they could pray. The God who was once believed in as the unchanging, eternal, unitary center of all things has simply disappeared from the reality scale of men who have come to value change, and whose experience is pluralistic and relative. A religion calling for human surrender to the will of this God no longer appeals to men who believe that, for better or worse, the course of life and this world lie in human hands. The worship of the churches seems hollow to such persons, not because it is in archaic language, not because the forms of that worship are out of date, but simply because worship is an activity which presupposes traditional theism. You can't very well worship if you do not think there is anything there to worship. The crisis of worship in the churches is only a symptom of the more fundamental crisis of faith.

Many of those who may be thought of as radical Christians still find that they wish to speak of God in some sense, whether as some unfalsifiable and therefore pragmatically insignificant Ground of all Being, or as a Pickwickian image or ideal. It would seem probable, however, in the light of the history of theism over the past three centuries and in the light of the elements of contemporary consciousness discussed, that this sort of vestigial theism (which is no real theism at all) will seem less and less helpful. This is all the more likely for the Christian who takes an increasing interest in the radical movements in our society, since the more he participates in these movements, the more he will share in the self-awareness underlying them.

If this is how the radical Christian has come to where he is, why, it must be asked, has he not gone the last step? Why does he still consider himself a Christian? Is it not logical, after what has happened to him, that he simply leave behind his Christian past as something outgrown? Why does he still use biblical terms and refer to the biblical story when he no longer can believe in the existence of the God of that story nor in its adequacy as a true story of the events it purports to present? If he once identified himself and his place in the world by reference to that story, but has now come to question so much in it because he so largely identifies himself in the world by reference to a newer story of human liberation, why go on telling the old story at all? If the old story is not true, if it is really a human story after all, then should it not properly be filed away with all the other human stories, no doubt a part of our past, but surely not immune to the critical and skeptical view with which we look at all old stories? It may well be that if this story was the one with which we were brought up (in contrast, say, to the stories of the Buddha with which we might have been brought up had we been born Indians, or the story of witches with which some of our ancestors were brought up, or the stories of the Greek gods with which our more distant ancestors were brought up), then we might perhaps have a certain nostalgia for our past. But surely if we once heard and told some such story as a way to understand our life in the world, that was because we thought it was true. If we now have found that our supposedly true story is a myth, is in important respects a fairy story, does it make sense to go on telling it? At the very least, we shall surely have to tell it in another way, once we realize that it is a story. The biographical answer as to why the new Christian, the non-theistic Christian, still wants in some way to retell the biblical story may be of psychological interest, but it does not answer the question of whether he should continue to tell the story. It may be true that we are in part determined by our past, but it is precisely characteristic of contemporary consciousness that we do not think we have to be determined by our past — and that we should ask whether we ought to listen to our past, and if so, to which parts of it.

On the other hand, these questions, fair as they are, might ask the impossible by presuming to speak for a radicality which feels that to be fully radical is to cut oneself off from all the past. To be a radical, in one important sense of the word, is to go to the roots of the matter, not to cut off the roots. To pretend to be totally free of the past is both naive and romantic. Demands for some imagined total elimination of the roots of the past are not to be taken seriously.

Since the radical Christian is aware that he does have roots and a past, and since, with his contemporaries, he regards these roots critically, yet knows that they form part of the material from which he must fashion his future, we can begin to see why he does not throw the whole story away, why he tells it in his own non-theistic way as a story of human imagination and hopes, as a human story of men who were driven on in history by a vision, a vision which they spoke of in theistic terms, but a vision which he thinks can also be told non-theistically, or humanly. For the new Christian, that story and its vision serve to supply words and imagery warning him that much that passes as *radically* new and revolutionary in

the world today is inadequate to much of human experience,
as well as naive about its own originality.

There is no denying that men have told other stories than
those of Adam and Eve, or the Tower of Babel, to remind
themselves that men are less than perfect. It is also true that
we can make the point without resorting to stories. The
human problem may be dramatic, but does it have to be
expressed in dramatic form, that is, as a story? I see no logical
necessity for the story form, but I remark simply that we
humans appear to be prone to tell stories as part of our way
of expressing who we are and of trying to convey to each
other how we see our lives in the world.[3] Perhaps we can say
that men tell stories because they have pasts. The very ambiguity latent in any well-told story is itself one of the reasons
why stories do the job for us. You don't have to see the point
of the story, just as you don't have to see the point of living.
The hearer must make his own interpretation. The story is
as flexible and as open-ended as human life itself, which makes
it an appropriate form for sharing our visions and hopes about
human life.[4]

Moreover, stories are flexible in the sense that they are
always being retold. As we have come to tell also the newer
story of the rise of science, industry, and technology, of the
expansion of learning and the building of our new age, we
are led to recast older stories. Specifically, the old story of
the Bible, which seemed to men once to have been a story
about God, is being retold more and more today as a story
about men, men who admittedly believed things we don't,
but men who interest us humanly, even if we cannot share
many of their beliefs. They interest us because of what we
can share with them, and because they remind us of the ambiguities in that other, newer story of modern man, and ask
us if we really believe all of that one either!

The radical Christians, whose situation I am exploring,
are certainly doing what Alasdair MacIntyre says they are
doing: "retaining a religious vocabulary emptied of belief-

content,"[5] and the sooner that is seen and acknowledged, the sooner we can move on to the interesting question of why they do this and what function it serves. Yet, MacIntyre is not quite on to what is going on here. Radical Christians are not simply retaining a religious vocabulary emptied of belief-content: they are in fact trying to adapt a religious vocabulary emptied of theistic belief-content to another purpose, or at least to a purpose other than the expression of theistic belief, leaving aside the question whether that really was its older purpose. They are in fact changing religious vocabulary, which is to say, they are changing religion. They are seeking something which, in the future, and indeed for many already, may well not be called a religion at all. Not being primarily interested in the name, I would put it this way: they are seeking to adapt some or much of the language of religion to satisfy a cultural need to which MacIntyre has also pointed: the need for a vocabulary for expressing our beliefs about how we are in the world.

Radicals of more sorts than the religious variety have seen the ambiguity of the cultural shift through which we have been and still are passing. To participate positively in the movement of one's culture, but to do so critically, seems as good a way as any of defining our task today. As we do this, we are aware to some extent that we are fashioning, or trying to fashion, a new world, a new style of life, and new institutional arrangements that will be less oppressive than those of the past. Many of us would say that that past suffered from too heteronomous criteria of critical judgment, whether it was the heteronomy of theism or of materialism, of God, or of science. The images around which we wish to understand our life in the world and the world which we are working for are human. The vocabulary for these images is all there in the only language we have, our human language, but we have not yet found the combination of words we are looking for.

Those who are Christians and involved in this enterprise, are, not surprisingly, trying to adapt some of the things they have learned from the religious story to this larger task. As they try to steer their way through the ambiguous elements in the self-awareness they share with so many who do not tell the religious story, it must seem at times that they are "retaining a religious vocabulary emptied of belief-content." They are indeed, but they do so for understandable reasons, and it may yet lead them to find the words they seek. Their need for the words to say who they are and how they are in the world is a need, a deep need, of our whole society. There is nothing distinctive about the problem the new Christian is up against. If there is anything that does distinguish him, it is not already discovered and formulated beliefs, such as those which distinguish the theist from others. It is rather the fact that he finds important the human images and metaphors in the biblical story as potential leads for saying where he is at this point in his search for the words to say what this human experiment is all about. That last phrase is not yet the one he wants. Maybe it would be a bit better to say that he wants to find the way in which to tell the human story. But then, if we had found how to say this, our radical Christians would not be in the situation they now are.

NOTES

1. I wish to express my indebtedness here, and at other places to be noted, to Alasdair MacIntyre's "The Debate about God: Victorian Relevance and Contemporary Irrelevance," in *The Religious Significance of Atheism*, by A. MacIntyre and Paul Ricoeur (New York: Columbia University Press, 1969).

2. I owe this provocative formulation of the problem to Professor R. M. Hare.

3. Cf. Ignatio Silone, "The Choice of Comrades," *Encounter*, vol. 3, no. 6 (December 1954), p. 28.

4. Giving reasons for why we speak as we do, why we do what we do with language, is a way of giving reasons for why we live as we do. That is an odd business. What counts as a reason for being the sort of animal who tells stories, who engages in this act of the imagination (among others), as a way of being what we call human?

5. MacIntyre, *op. cit.*, p. 53.

THE THEOLOGY OF RADICAL SECULARITY: A SECULAR CRITIQUE

Thomas Dean

The most creative and promising movement in theology today is the theology of radical secularity.[1] This is not a temporary fad or a passing trend but the theology of the foreseeable future. Most important for the present purpose, it is the theology best qualified for a dialogue with the new Marxist humanism and with secular thought in general.[2]

It should be argued here, however, that this radical reconstruction of Christian theology has not succeeded in overcoming the objections of either Marxism or contemporary philosophy. To show this, we shall consider not only matters of detail and inner consistency but the prior question of whether secular theology (because it is secular *theology*) is possible at all. More specifically, we shall not argue the weaker thesis that all such theologies to date have failed, but the stronger claim that any such attempt must necessarily fail.[3]

This proposition may be demonstrated in a number of ways, corresponding to the variety of arguments advanced on behalf of a radically secular theology. The arguments from (1) history, (2) the future, (3) the world, (4) man, and (5) God will be examined in turn, after which (6) the argument from the future will be revisited.

THE ARGUMENT FROM HISTORY

One of the basic questions which the secular critic has of a distinctively Christian approach to secularity is one which Jürgen Moltmann himself asks as a theologian: "Why dialogue precisely with *these texts* and with *this past?*"[4] As long as the theologian refuses to confront this preliminary question, he is still living uncritically from the interest of his tradition. However "radical" his posture, he is merely continuing "traditionalism" by other means.[5] Behind the more obvious apologetic issue: "How can and should one understand the Christian tradition today?" there lies this even more radical question: "*Why* is one compelled to preach precisely those texts, to understand and believe them?"[6] Why are we compelled to view our contemporary reality primarily (if not exclusively) in the light of the biblical perspective?[7]

The secular Christian answer to this question rests on the argument from history, that is, on descriptive and normative precedent: Christianity got there first.[8] The Judeo-Christian tradition, as even its Marxist critics agree, was of decisive influence in the formation of the western perspective on man and the world. Hence, it is normative not only for our understanding of the past of that culture, but for the development of its future possibilities. Since this argument rests on certain factual as well as interpretive assumptions, we must look to the evidence offered in their support.

"Theology," says Moltmann, "can teach only on the ground of the word given in tradition."[9] The first question, therefore, is: what is this tradition? Simply as a request for information, the question immediately leads one into a maze of complexities. It not only involves the difficulty of getting clear about the exact nature of the biblical origins. It also presents the problem of assessing the tradition's subsequent growth and development in all its continuity and discontinuity, and with its accretion of the foreign and the new, both in church and secular history. When to this factual request is added a demand for the clarification of such normative terminology as "decisive," "definitive," "unique," "distinctive," "essential," and so on, then the size of the task is apparent.

To show the nature and importance of the issue at stake, two cases crucial to the radical Christian use of the argument from history shall be examined. The key historical figure and symbol for the secular theologian is Jesus Christ, his cross and resurrection. It is claimed that Jesus is, actually and symbolically, "a political, in fact, a revolutionary figure."[10] The cross and resurrection of Jesus are the source and continuing inspiration of a "political," more specifically, a "revolutionary historical" hermeneutic.[11] It is in the life and teaching of Jesus, or in the spirit of Christ, that the secular Christian finds the call for a radical break with the old secular (social and political) order and the construction of a radically new order.

The radical theologian is also concerned to affirm the independent integrity of a "secular" Christianity, that is, to show that the Judeo-Christian tradition, independent of its relationship to modern, secular culture, has its own, biblical resources for a theoretical and practical promotion of secular man's struggle to create his own future. As Karl Rahner contends: "Christianity as the religion of the absolute future . . . is not a modernist interpretation of Christianity or one which arose only from contact with Marxism."[12]

Now both these claims must be brought into serious question in light of everything else known about the origins of our distinctively modern, secular, and revolutionary self-consciousness. To begin with the second claim: some of the radical theologians themselves are willing to admit, in contrast to Rahner, that secular theology has learned, and can still learn, much from secular society and culture, and not merely in the "accidentals" of their faith. According to Harvey Cox and Richard Shaull, for example, Christian theology today *needs* secular thought and praxis in order to "regain" the "essentials" of its faith.[13]

But there is an even more damaging point to be made. The claim that Christianity does not need to be interpreted with the help of contemporary culture because it is the spiritual progenitor of modern secular and revolutionary consciousness is, to put it briefly, simply not true. As Hannah Arendt convincingly shows, the origins of both modern man's secular consciousness and his revolutionary praxis are to be found in the rise of modern economic, social, and political life, in the age of absolutism and the two great revolutions at the end of the eighteenth century.[14]

The same must be said for the related claim that the notion of history, with its linear development and element of inexpungeable novelty, is Judeo-Christian in origin. As has been shown elsewhere in the present volume,[15] even where the Christian philosophy of history succeeded in partially comprehending the novelty and unrepeatability of the Christ-event, its understanding of both sacred and secular history remained for the most part bound within the cycles of antiquity. With Arendt we must conclude that "the best one can say in favor of this theory is that it needed modernity to liberate the revolutionary germ of the Christian faith, which obviously is begging the question."[16]

Then what about the claim that Jesus has a political-revolutionary significance for secular Christianity? Both to those who argue, roughly, that Jesus was really the first Com-

munist, that he struggled for social justice, and that Marxism
is really a secularized version of Christianity, and to those
who, conceding that this was not the case, still urge his spiritual or symbolic significance for the modern revolutionary
impetus, it must be pointed out that the very quest for a
"revolutionary" Jesus is misleading and misguided. It is misleading because it assumes that more historical information
might serve to settle the argument, whereas in fact the question of historical influence is much more complex. It is misguided because it inevitably leads to a reduction of the
historical element to a bare factual vehicle for the convey-
ance of larger, more malleable "symbolic" truths, whereas
it is the actual, practico-historical content of the Christ-event
that the problem is all about.

Whether the argument for the revolutionary significance
of Christ appeals to actual fact or to symbolic truth, therefore, it cannot be judged persuasive. At best, the radical Christian is entitled to conclude that Jesus, as a religious leader,
offered important pre-revolutionary insights; but, as the Marxist would remind him, it is "opposition, political opposition"
that must be rendered unto Caesar. Hence, the radical theologian would do better to find other revolutionary examples
than Jesus.[17]

The reliance of the secular Christian upon this particular
case provides a clear illustration of the way in which the
argument from history can turn into a two-edged sword. If
an historian were to ask what it was about Jesus that was so
new, so totally unique, what it was that made him for Christians the "hinge of history," perhaps the least controversial
reply would be that, in terms of his novelty, historical precedents can be found throughout the Jewish tradition, not
to mention the parallels in the other great religious and moral
traditions. His decisive significance for the early Christians,
therefore, lay rather in the fact that in Jesus the eschatological
timetable was advanced another step. Having been partially
and proleptically realized (i.e., secularized) in his person, the

Kingdom was then, through faith, extended in the lives of the Christian community.

But the force of this historical observation leads the secular thinker who finds contemporary meaning in the biblical events to the opposite conclusion. For a Marxist humanist like Ernst Bloch, the proper conclusion is that it is our task to complete what was partially and only indirectly begun in the Judeo-Christian faith, namely, the genuinely secular realization of what the Christians referred to mythologically as the Kingdom of God. This would lead to abolishing, not perpetuating, the religious expression of faith in order to promote true secular humanity.

From a radically secular perspective, therefore, the radical Christian attempt to establish the primacy of the Christ-event and the Christian historical tradition for the revolutionary realization of human (secular) emancipation seems an exercise in futility and self-contradiction. It is an effort to preserve the old story, the expectations of an ancient world-view (eschatology), under the same name but in a totally different setting. To the extent that it succeeds, with the help of the novel concepts and historical praxis of the modern, secular world, it acknowledges, in effect, the primacy (if not the chronological priority) of the latter; and thus, in fact, it fails.[18]

The attempt at an historical defense of the secular Christian claim to primacy in the "essentials" as well as priority in time vis-à-vis secular self-consciousness is complex and questionable enough. When there is added the evaluative claim that the biblical tradition represents a continuing source of inspiration for contemporary social and political struggle, the radical Christian position seems to make the qualitative leap from improbability to impossibility. At the very least, the argument from history must be judged inconclusive.

But perhaps this is as it should be; perhaps it is inherent in the nature of this particular discussion. For as a theology oriented primarily to the future, secular Christianity itself reminds us that the answer to the question of the uniqueness or superiority of the Christian perspective should not be sought exclusively in a consideration of its past history. It can only be found by expanding our search to take in the eschatological dimension as well, for history, including the past, can finally be understood only under the aspect of its future. Here, rather than in a catalog of past events, is where the decisive answer to the secular hope of man resides. The same applies a fortiori to modern secular and revolutionary self-consciousness. Proof or disproof of the Christian origins of secularity tells us nothing definitive about the future possibilities of either those origins or their supposed derivatives.[19]

THE ARGUMENT FROM THE FUTURE

There are at least two reasons why a radical Christian eschatology might consider itself superior to any secular form of utopian ideology: it speaks of and promises more, yet it knows and endangers us less.

The logical consequences of this paradoxical conjunction of arguments, when spelled out, appear contradictory. If secular hope seems to project itself too far, it is immediately attacked for failing to respect the limits of human understanding, for attempting to envision what can never be seen from the present vantage-point. But if secular hope is scaled down to a limited, human-sized projection, it is immediately faulted for its inability or failure to speak to "first and last things." And yet, when pressed for information or criteria concerning an alternative eschatological vision or certitude, the theologian becomes reticent, contenting himself with negative, cautionary notes or, at most, appealing to faith in that which is "unseen." Attributing to his secular opponent an inability to achieve a self-critical and self-transcendent vision of the future, he declares his own ideology off limits when the same demand is made on it. Thus, what would appear to a secular critic as the tactical inferiority of Christianity's epistemic claim upon the future is mysteriously con-

verted into an impregnable methodological asset: the
Christian vision of man's absolute future in God "cannot be
confirmed within history but can only be accepted in faith."[20]

The underlying difficulty with this line of argument is
that it leaves us without any criteria (save, possibly, negative
ones) for distinguishing warranted from unwarranted projections of human hope. It rests in a profound ambivalence,
a refusal to concede that a radically secular vision of the
future could avoid confusing the question of the world and
of man as a whole with either specific data about man and
the world or limited, planned projections of specific, "innerworldly" futures.[21] For a contemporary secular perspective,
one that is increasingly capable of self-criticism and self-
transcendence, this traditional theological maneuver with its
claim to another, higher form of insight and self-authentica-
tion, simply fails to convince. Its appeal to an irreducible
element of "mystery" and "paradox" looks like the introduction of mystification and self-contradiction instead — a patent
weakness, not a hidden strength of the position.

The argument from the future thus leaves several questions: Is the theologian's suspicion justified? If so, on what
grounds does the theologian (who here makes a claim from
which the secular thinker abstains) justify his own claim to
have a superior vision, one which does apply to "first and
last" things, to the world and to man as a whole? If not, what
does this mean for the possibility of a secular vision of the
future and what does it signify for theology's putative eschatological guarantees?

The fact is that the radical Christian vision of the future
is riddled with metaphysical and epistemological ambiguities,
whose consequence is an ambivalent commitment to the
revolutionary cause of transforming the secular world.

THE ARGUMENT FROM THE WORLD

The ambivalence of the radical Christian attitude to the
secular world shows itself in a reluctance to identify with,

and to commit itself fully to, the concrete work of human emancipation. It is capable of doing so "radically" . . . up to a point. For its concern for the world can never be more than "provisional" or "penultimate." Despite its radicalism, it is (in a vertical and not simply a temporal sense) "in" but not "of" the world. Its ultimate source and ultimate hope lie elsewhere.[22]

Karl Rahner tells us, for example: "Regarding the material content of this [innerworldly] future, Christianity has just as little to say. It does not set up an innerworldly ideal for the future; it makes no prognosis and does not bind man to any determinate goals for an innerworldly future."[23] And yet, at the same time, the theologian can add that, because it is a religion of the *absolute* future, which is "neutral" to all our particular futures, Christianity is therefore "liberating in regard to man's individual and collective innerworldly aims," that, in fact, it "confers a final radical seriousness to the work of building an innerworldly future."[24] Because of its "decisive objection" to every secular vision of utopia, Christian eschatology makes possible "a radical humanism . . . more human than its autonomous counterpart. . . ."[25]

Now there is a serious problem here. It must be granted that this refusal to identify the absolute with any particular is the Judeo-Christian tradition's way of proscribing the fashioning of false idols from human hopes. But Christianity has always been unequivocally historical and has not hesitated from earliest times on to take stands and make commitments (for the most part, establishmentarian) to specific historical programs and goals. In this period of history, at this particular juncture in the discussion with Marxist humanism, men's need today is to hear the opposite sort of "glad tidings." We need to hear that our deepest dreams and highest aspirations are relevant to a world come-of-age, that our most urgent "utopias" are more capable than ever before of realization.

Hence secular man will no longer allow the realization of his hopes and dreams to be declared forever beyond his this-

worldly reach. He must refuse the priestly illogic that would
have him move from saying "no" to some particular stage of
this secular world, to a refusal to say "yes" to the secular
world as a whole. The ultimate thrust of a radical perspective
on secularity runs directly counter to this final reservation of
the secular theologian, for its explicit concern is to find "a
way of transcending the present world while remaining firmly
within it."[26]

A radically secular perspective on man's commitment to
the world demands of contemporary thought two things: full
theoretical acknowledgment of secular man's hard-won capacity for self-critical self-transcendence, and a defense of his
ability to affirm this finite, temporal, historical world as the
true field of his creative activity on behalf of man's future.
Anything less will necessarily rely upon an appeal to man's
weakness, ignorance, and fear, and hence can only provision-
ally affirm his knowledge, courage, and strength. To speak to
men's weakness is one thing, but to play on it, to take advantage of it, to claim to have the only guarantee for overcoming it, is another matter altogether.

THE ARGUMENT FROM MAN

The same ambivalence or illogic which characterizes the
eschatological expectations and secular commitment of radical
Christianity is also found in its argument from man. There
is an implicit contradiction between its celebration of secular
man come-of-age and its underlying appeal to man's weakness (as distinct from his finitude, for that, too, is a double-
edged sword).

Moltmann, one of the leading advocates of "the revolutionary realization of human fortune," bases the superiority
of Christian anthropology over Ernst Bloch's Marxist humanism on the latter's inability to provide spiritual reassurance
and an eschatological guarantee concerning "the regions over
which nothingness holds sway and where human beings ex-

perience suffering and death." Moltmann contends that Bloch's ontology of "not-yet-being" "comprehends nothingness only to the extent that the courage to hope can 'do something'; it cannot apply hope to no-longer-being."[27] Christian anthropology, unlike secular forms of humanism, is more "radical" because it holds out the promise of a "greater future" than the one secular man can hope for on his own. It promises to liberate man not only from this or that particular (finite) threat of "non-being," but from "the power of transitoriness" itself. Rahner, an equally strong defender of the superiority of Christian humanism, analogously argues that "no economic change or social system can prevent man from an experiential awareness of his limit in death, thereby — though not only thereby — placing his whole being in question."[28]

Now while this may be true in general, it must be asked whether the only conclusion that necessarily follows is the theologian's: namely, that man on his own is unable to answer this question for himself. This is not to suggest, as Bonhoeffer sometimes seems to do, that the existential problems of James's "sick souls" are to be swept under the rug as a secular embarrassment. Such experiences are a necessary part of the total condition of man. The question, however, is whether it requires the theologian's remedy to face them.

This brings up the secular Christian's second anthropological move: its radical reconstruction of the traditional understanding of man's freedom and God's grace. For Rahner, "grace is nothing other than God's gift of himself as the absolute future . . . as the future of the world."[29] Even on this revisionist or "futural" reading, however, divine grace is necessary to free man to realize his "essential" humanity in a way he would not otherwise be able to do. He is not free himself to initiate or bring to fulfillment the process of genuine human emancipation. In other words, the inner logic of this Christian anthropology, even its revised, secular form, is still dependent for its sense upon the traditional meta-

physics of "essence" and "existence," a distinction derived
from Greek rather than biblical sources, from an anthropology
whose model of human existence is conceptually derived from
the quite different logic of thingly existence.[30]

The modern experience of man's autonomy and capacity
for historical initiative requires a totally different ontological
foundation. It demands an interpretation that views man's
worldly being as identical with radical freedom and self-
transcendence (human existence as "ek-sistence," not a mode
of the medieval *existentia*), one which views the "essence"
and thus the "necessities" of man's being as constituted by,
not the determinants of, his concrete free activity. In such
an anthropology, it would be impossible to drive a metaphysical wedge between man's essential possibilities and his
actual historical praxis. For a radically secular perspective,
man's "essential possibilities" are not something "already
there" in *potentia*, waiting to be liberated by God or man;
they are imaginative projections constituting a summons to
the ongoing task of the historical creation of man by man
himself.

There are two ways to read the lesson of human finitude,
therefore, only one of which requires a theological assist. Moltmann agrees with contemporary secular thought that "our
knowledge . . . has a transcendent and provisional character
marked by promise and expectation, in virtue of which it
recognizes the open horizon of the future of reality and thus
preserves the finitude of human experience."[31] Man's finitude
is his capacity for self-transcendence. But this, it turns out, is
not enough for the theologian desirous of providing guarantees for the realization of man's highest hopes. It is Shaull,
astonishingly, who thinks he has adequately characterized the
two alternatives with regard to a radical humanism by ac-
counting for them in this way:

> this radical transcendence and transgression could have
> only one of two sources. It could come as the result of

ascribing infinite value to one aspect of finite reality. . . .
the second alternative . . . reverses this whole process. The
object of loyalty is not some element of the finite which
has been absolutized, but the Creator who relativizes and
at the same time sustains all created reality.[32]

But are we really offered two alternatives here, or is it
not rather just one choice presenting two different faces, a
"good," theistic aspect and a "bad," anti-theistic aspect? Is
it not possible to conceive another possibility, namely, a
genuinely *second* alternative — an ontology of human finitude
which is precisely that? If so, we must first take explicit account of the final argument of radical Christianity, one we
have been considering implicitly all along, the linchpin of this
as of any other theology.

THE ARGUMENT FROM GOD

For the theologian, as for the radical secularist, the fundamental question underlying this entire discussion is, finally,
"why God?"[33] For Harvey Cox, this question is:

Does man's unfaltering hope for a more human and
just world have any grounding in reality itself? Is there
reason to believe the developing universe itself sustains
the human aspiration it seems to elicit, or is man's hope
only his own wishful projection, something to which both
history and the cosmos remain supremely indifferent? It is
the contention of Biblical faith that there is a mystery
from which man emerges, a reality that summons him to
anguished freedom and joyous responsibility, a real ground
for the hopes man entertains for himself and his race.[34]

Similarly, for Shaull, "human life is seen as most human when
it is lived in response to a higher loyalty than self, and expresses the trust that reality — coming-to-be — is ultimately
favorable to man."[35] The secularist, for his part, might agree

with the theologian that "reality — coming-to-be" probably
does indeed carry greater ontological weight than "man," but
he nevertheless feels compelled to ask whether we are justified
in calling that oblong blur "God."

The theologian's "proof" seems to rest on two presuppositions: the theism-relative or ontologically dependent status
of atheism, and the impossibility of "radical transcendence"
on any other than theistic terms. Let us consider each in turn.

One of the standard theological criticisms of atheistic
humanism is that it is conceptually and existentially dependent
upon the theism it rejects. For Moltmann, " 'atheism' is always a relative concept . . . it opposes concepts and notions
which describe God as . . .", etc.[36] Even when proclaimed in
the name of a prior and positive commitment to man, atheism
is (if one looks closely enough at its concept of man) parasitic
for its content and significance upon the theism it attempts
to replace. Atheism is always anti-theism, theism-relative humanism, and thus bound negatively but dialectically by the
rules of the theist's "onto-theo-logic."[37] The favorite contemporary illustration of this thesis among theologians is, of
course, Sartre's "anguished freedom," which views man's being
as "useless passion," a futile striving to realize the impossible
ideal of "being-in-itself for-itself," that is, "to be God."

This highly subtle put-down of secular humanism is supported by the further claim that a radical doctrine of transcendence is, in any case, impossible to articulate in immanentalist
terms. Over against the Marxist humanist attempt to form-
ulate such a notion, Moltmann argues that "the apocalyptic
content of the Bible . . . can be brought into the dialectical
and historical process of the mediation of man and nature only
if that which occurs without any mediation — the sudden and
transcendent end as understood in the Bible — is translated
into what is subject to mediation: transcendental immanence
without transcendence." In this process the divine reality
emerges much diminished; in fact, it is "reduced to a nuclear
immanence within matter." Thus, what seemed to the Marxist

an act of demythologization necessary to activate secular hope appears to the eye of the theologian to be a remythologization of nature, a reintroduction of the divine mystification into the natural process from whence it had originally been removed ("desacralized") by the biblical account of Creation.[38]

Here the theology of radical secularity, supported by the ontologies of Ernst Bloch, Alfred North Whitehead, and others, moves onto the theoretical offensive. To the extent that the atheist's opposition to Christian theism rests on a rejection of the mythological language of the Bible or the metaphysical concepts of a theology grounded in the absolute and unchanging Being of classical metaphysics, his objections are well taken. The new theologians agree that acceptance of either the language of myth or the language of classical onto-theo-logy entails a denial of the full autonomy and significance of the secular world. But rejection of "that peculiar combination of myth and traditional metaphysics called classical theism" does not entitle the atheist to take the further step of concluding that it must and can reject all forms of theism.[39]

What entitles the secular theologian to make this claim? The exegetical rediscovery of the dynamic God of biblical faith, yes. But more important — since the mythological language of the Bible can be a stumbling-block — is the discovery of a new ontology whose basic categories are those of temporality and historicity, a metaphysics which places relativity and the affirmation of change in the very heart of Being itself.[40] This new ontology is what informs Shaull's and Cox's view of ultimate reality as a process of "coming-to-be"; it is what grounds Braaten's and Moltmann's claim that "the future [is] a divine mode of being."[41] Accordingly, if God's "eternity" is understood as his "eminent temporality" under the primary aspect of its open futurity, then God's "Being," far from alienating man from his secular self-consciousness and his this-worldly being, in fact reaffirms that secularity in its very ontological depths.[42]

For the secular critic, however, this problem is not yet resolved. Just how do these categories of temporality and relativity apply to our concept of reality as a whole, to the totality of being, and to God as the highest being? Schubert Ogden replies that, for a secular metaphysician like Heidegger, and presumably for Bloch and Whitehead too, "finitude is seen . . . to consist not in temporality and relatedness as such, but in the limited mode of these perfections appropriate to our being as men." Therefore, if temporality and relativity are in their "primal forms" constitutive of being itself, then "God's uniqueness is to be construed not simply by denying them, but by conceiving them in their infinite mode through the negation of their limitations as we experience them in ourselves."[43]

But this answer simply raises further questions. Is the logic of this move from the finite to the infinite, even in its new form, acceptable? Does this new concept of God really overcome the alienating effect upon secular man of the traditional concept?

The metaphysical use of this reconstructed concept of God as eminent temporality (futurity), despite its categorial novelty, is subject to the same Kantian strictures which applied to the older, classical metaphysics of God. The radical conversion of the predicates of divine being from immutability to relationality, from "eternal presence" to "open futurity," should not obscure the fact that the theologian is still trying to retain, to "prove," the subject of these predicates. The difficulty lies not in the notion of God's being as *temporal*, but in its *infinite* temporality — a leap which post-Kantian metaphysics, processive or otherwise, is not licensed to take.

The question, therefore, is a more serious one. It is whether the underlying logic of either the theistic or the anti-theistic position makes any sense at all. After Hume and Kant, does it make sense any longer to use such phrases as "the totality of being" (Moltmann), "reality itself" (Cox), "reality

— coming-to-be" (Shaull), "the world and man as a whole" (Rahner), "the ultimate metaphysical reality" (Ogden), "the absolute future" (Rahner)? If these terms are to have any theistic significance, then they must also have an ontologically explanatory and referential function, and clearly, that is how these theologians intend them to be taken. But in fact such terms at best have only a general methodological sense within a descriptive metaphysics. The attempt to use them as quasi-referential terms in the service of a theistic "proof" still generates today, as in Kant's time, those transcendental illusions which we have come to associate with theological speculation.

There is the further problem. Even this new, temporal concept of God's being, contrary to the claims of its most revolutionary-minded adherents, does not fully overcome the alienating effect of the traditional notion of God. Again, the radical reconstruction of the divine predicates in line with the general features of man's secular being might lead one to think that the Marxist's suspicions on this score could be overcome. (The hidden assumption, apparently, is that Christians, by yielding to Marxists on the *predicates* of ultimate reality, might in turn succeed in encouraging the Marxist to yield to the Christian on the *divinity* of these predicates.) The problem from a radically secular perspective, however, is that the dispute over the predicates of the divine is not the chief issue. The Marxist was in any case already persuaded of the "dialectical" nature of ultimate reality. No, his fundamental concern is rather with the divinity of these predicates, specifically with the theologian's assumption that without this divine backing these predicates would lose their ultimate significance for man's being.[44]

Ogden's "derivation" of the predicates of God's being from the predicates of man's being ("by conceiving them in their infinite mode through the negation of their limitations as we experience them in ourselves") neatly revives the anthropological-ontological grounds for the Feuerbachian and

Marxist animus *against* "the argument from God." Again "God" becomes the alienated and alienating expression of man's finite perfections. Claiming to be their ground and guarantee, it in fact infinitely *negates* them. In addition, "God" is now more subtly totalitarian than when the predicates of divine being differed in content from their human counterparts. With this similarity in predicates, the remaining difference in their extension — God as the eminent sublimation of human transience — seems even more oppressive. Thus, the closer this theology of radical secularity comes to our human secularity, the further away it is, as *theology*, from a truly *radical*, that is, *human* secularity.

As Marx concluded in his dialogue with the left-wing theologians of his day, so too today it would seem that the theology of radical secularity must be stood on its head if its genuinely radical and secular truth is to be realized. For by insisting upon a doctrine of God as the highest being and a priori guarantee (even as eminent temporality) of an open future, the radical theologians are every bit as much transcendental-historical idealists as Marx's Hegelian partners in dialogue. Their ability to affirm and work for the realization of man's secular hopes is itself "grounded" in a prior adherence to that God whose eternity (ideality) is to be thought of as "the future of every past, the future of every present, as ontologically prior in his futurity to every event and epoch of the remotest distance from us."[45] If "idealism" is that view of the world, whether static or processive, which sees finite being as a priori subsumed under an infinite and eternal (spiritual or ideal) being, then the theology of radically secular Christianity, too, is an Idealism.[46]

From a radically secular perspective, the truth of "materialism," that is, a finite ontology of radical secularity, can no longer be denied. The evidence for this theoretic claim is already forthcoming on the level of contemporary secular praxis. This will become clearer if we reconsider the practical implications of the argument from the future.

THE ARGUMENT FROM THE FUTURE REVISITED

The argument from the future states that the question of the relative merits of the Christian and the secular humanist (specifically, Marxist) visions of man and the world is to be settled not simply by a comparison of their past performances, but by an estimate of the respective futures they propose and their effectiveness in bringing them about. Hence the events, the concepts, and the visions of Christian eschatology and Marxist utopian ideology ought not to be taken as the objects, laws, or predictions of a speculative science of history. They are, according to Moltmann, "not so much generic concepts for the subsuming of known reality as rather dynamic functional concepts whose aim is the future transformation of reality." These anthropological and cosmological visions are "sketches for the future," whose inner logic (the "projective" logic of promise and demand) drives them out of ideality into the realm of praxis. To understand and evaluate them properly, one must judge them in terms of their capacity to bring about their own "abolition" as merely *speculative ideas* by securing their "realization" as *practical forces* in the transformation of the world.[47]

If a theology of radical secularity is to preserve itself from the charge of being a new variation on idealism, it must indicate in what concrete respects Christian eschatology is not simply a speculative vision but one which holds its own with Marxism as "a practical attitude to the future."[48] Is Christian eschatology capable of demonstrating that, in this practico-historical sense, it too is a "materialism" rather than an "idealism"?

As soon as the question is put in this way, its answer must be readily apparent. For the truth is that, in terms of the several criteria by which the pragmatic or future-practical validity of the Christian vision might reasonably be judged — ideological content, practical analysis, historical initiative — the theology of radical secularity is the dependent rather than the creative partner in the dialogue with secular humanism.

Ideologically, one of the basic features of this theology is its appreciation of the essentially futural nature of being, its sense that the "essence" of something is not what it was or is, but what it has the capacity to become, what it can or will be. So there is something ironic, if not self-contradictory, in its attempt to ground both this insight and its defense of Christianity as essentially future-oriented in an appeal to the "essentials" "already there" in the biblical past. Thus Metz, apparently without reflecting on the internal logic of his claim, tells us that "contemporary man's orientation to the future . . . [is] grounded in the biblical faith. . . ."⁴⁹ By his own estimate, what Christianity "essentially" is, or even was, can be determined only (and even then, never definitively) by what it yet can be. The "grounds" of contemporary (or even biblical) man's orientation to the future can only be that open-ended future itself. Have these theologians really considered the *radical* consequences of their own ideological affirmations?

The fact is that this theology of the radically open, the new, the revolutionary, is incapable of acknowledging the coming-into-being of the totally new unless it can show it to have been anticipated by and grounded in the "essentials" of the biblical perspective. Theology, as we recall Moltmann saying, "can only teach on the ground of the word given in the tradition." In short, it can only retell the *old* story; it cannot entertain, let alone conceive, a radically *new* one. But (our second irony) Christian eschatology itself has had to rely increasingly on the thought and praxis of the secular world, not only to comprehend the *novum* but to understand and gain a hearing for its retelling of its own story. Thus it is that the theology of radical secularity comes to find itself "announcing to the secular world, as though by way of a discovery, what the secular world has been announcing to it for a rather long time."⁵⁰

Practically, the theology of secularity maintains the fiction of its continuing "effectiveness" either by evacuating its social and political vision of its theistic content or, more frequently, by keeping to the level of extreme imaginative generality. Even then, in its dialogue with competing secular visions, it tends to view its role as primarily negative. The more "neutral" it can be vis-à-vis every particular this-worldly vision of the future, the better. The value of its "dynamic functional concepts" then reduces to that of a meta-reminder that we finite men ought not to absolutize our partial and relative visions. But this is a reminder that secular man, "radicalized" in his commitment to the future of this world by his experience of its twentieth-century horrors, is able to provide himself. There is no need to fall back on a theological interpretation of its truth.

Finally, insofar as the Christian vision is a theological world-view grounded in a religious way of life and concerned primarily with the activity, individual and collective, of Christians in their sociologically distinct roles as church-goers, prayers, and so on, it must be said that the historical initiative, the specific methods, tools, and institutions for the creation of man's future, have passed out of its hands into those of the secular world itself. The earthly future of man is no longer to be found in sole or even primary reliance upon the retelling and reliving of the old story, but in the disciplines and techniques, the visions and deeds, of the new story of secularity. The question for the future, therefore, is not whether theology can once again accommodate itself to secularity, but whether theology and religion in general can provide the secular world with specific thought and practice which will create the future. That, for the Marxist, is the final point of it all.

SOME TRANSITIONAL REMARKS

It is here that theology's prospects are dimmest. Since Hume and Kant, theism has not been a valid theoretical option as a world view; nor, since Marx, Nietzsche, and Freud, has religion really been a valid practical option as a way of life. Plainly, theological thought in the future cannot hope to be saved by an appropriation of secular thought. Nor can it expect to get past its secular hearers on the strength of such linguistic shockers as "Before God and with God we live without God" (Bonhoeffer) or "God is of no use whatever and that is why He is God" (Fontinell). The fact is that any presentation of theism which is able to gain a hearing from secular thought does so only by undergoing a transformation that empties it entirely of its theistic content.[51]

We are obliged to draw the logical conclusion and to take the final step: the thinking of the future demands a decisive, a *radical* break with theological thought as such. It calls for a radically different option, another kind of thinking altogether, one that is neither theistic nor anti-theistic. As with Marx, this thinking must not exhaust itself in the negation and destruction of religion; rather, it must clear the ground for a new, secular faith, a faith for the post-religious world.[52] It must deliberately reverse the previous direction of thought: instead of moving from secular thought back to its Greek or Christian ground, it must move forward from our classical and biblical heritage to create a new truth out of the revolutionary thought and praxis of our secular world. It is to this other way of thinking, this new ontology of radical secularity, that we must now turn.

NOTES

1. "Theology of radical secularity" is a loose cover for a number of contemporary theological efforts ranging from the non-theistic, ethical Christianity of Paul van Buren, the revolutionary theology of Richard Shaull, and the political or worldly theologies of Jürgen Moltmann and Johannes Metz, to the neo- or post-classical theologies of process and temporality in Karl Rahner, Leslie Dewart, Wolfhart Pannenberg, Schubert Ogden, et al. (For essays representative of these general tendencies, see Martin Marty and Dean Peerman, eds., New Theology No. 5 and No. 6 (New York, 1968 and 1969). Numerous and deep though their differences are, these theologies are united over against the classical theologies of the past by their renewed appreciation of the central rather than the marginal significance of biblical eschatology and by their shared affirmation of the emerging processive world view, the scientific and technological accomplishments, and the revolutionary sociopolitical praxis of modern, secular man. Drawing on philosophers like Whitehead and Wittgenstein, James and Dewey, Heidegger and Merleau-Ponty, they are participants in the shift "from permanence toward change, from the universal to the particular, from unity to plurality, from the absolute to the relative, and from passivity to activity" (P. van Buren, "Ethics and Secular Christianity," unpublished ms., p. 2) — that is, in the movement toward a "radical secularity" (a phrase intended to have both philosophical and sociopolitical connotations).

2. In contrast, say, with the existentialist individualism of the Bultmannian hermeneutic, the neo-orthodox "realism" of the Niebuhrians, or the earlier stages of "secular" or "radical" theology. A recent collection of discussions between Marxists and Christians is in Paul Oestreicher, ed., The Christian Marxist Dialogue (New York, 1969). The new Marxist humanism is represented in the work of such "revisionist" or neo-Marxist philosophers as Ernst Bloch, Roger Garaudy, Herbert Marcuse, Leszek Kolakowski, et al. The volume of essays edited by Erich Fromm (Socialist Humanism, Garden City, New York, 1965) shows that the new Marxist humanism, like the theology of radical secularity, is not a peripheral phase but the major direction of creative Marxist thought today.

3. Alasdair MacIntyre argues this same thesis in "The Debate about God: Victorian Relevance and Contemporary Irrelevance," in The Religious Significance of Atheism, by Alasdair MacIntyre and Paul Ricoeur (New York, 1969), p. 26.

4. Jürgen Moltmann, "Toward a Political Hermeneutic of the Gospel," New Theology No. 5, p. 69.

5. It is somewhat startling, therefore, to find van Buren saying that "the theologian cannot even begin to consider the question why it should be this book which is decisive for his work, why it should be this rather than some other book, for that would be to consider as a serious question of theology whether there ought to be theology at all" ("On Doing Theology" in Talk of God, Royal Institute of Philosophy Lectures, vol. 2, 1967–68 [London, 1969], p. 55). Either this is a harmless tautology ("By definition, theology cannot . . ."), in which case it does not constitute an answer to Moltmann's question; or it is a serious petitio principii. It is precisely the "secular" theologian, who shares the methods and world view of modern criticism, who should consider this the question with which to begin, if he is to gain a hearing for his theology at

all. He may prefer to regard this as a question for the "prolegomena" to theology, but this does not affect the basic issue — it merely renders it explicit. [It should be noted that in his essay in the present volume, van Buren does address himself to this particular objection. — Eds.]

6. Moltmann, "Political Hermeneutic," p. 69.

7. Thus, for van Buren, theology is "that activity of men struck by the biblical story, in which they undertake to revise continually the ways in which they say how things are with their present circumstances in the light of how they read that story" ("On Doing Theology," p. 53). The underlying assumption is that apologetics moves from the biblical to the contemporary, not (as a secular thinker might assume) vice versa.

8. Cf. Johannes Metz, cited in Ingo Hermann, "Total Humanism" (an extensive report on the Salzburg colloquium of Marxist and Christian thinkers), in *Is God Dead?* ed. J. B. Metz (New York, 1966), p. 166.

9. Jürgen Moltmann, *The Theology of Hope* (New York, 1967), p. 292.

10. As, for example, Richard Shaull claims in "Revolution: Heritage and Contemporary Option," in *Containment and Change*, by Carl Oglesby and Richard Shaull (New York, 1967), p. 228.

11. Moltmann, "Political Hermeneutic," pp. 77–81.

12. Karl Rahner, cited in Hermann, "Total Humanism," p. 168.

13. Harvey Cox, "Ernst Bloch and 'The Pull of the Future,'" *New Theology No. 5*, p. 196; Shaull, "Revolution," p. 213.

14. Hannah Arendt, *On Revolution* (New York, 1963), pp. 18–19, 21.

15. Cf. John Raines, "From Passive to Active Man."

16. Arendt, *On Revolution*, pp. 19–20.

17. Steve Weissman makes this point in "New Left Man Meets The Dead God," *New Theology No. 5*, pp. 23, 41–42.

18. Cf. MacIntyre, "The Debate About God," pp. 26–27.

19. Cf. Moltmann, *Theology of Hope*, pp. 28, 81–82.

20. Gilbert Mury's comment on Rahner and Metz, in Ingo Hermann, "Total Humanism," p. 167; cf. Moltmann, *Theology of Hope*, pp. 58, 78.

21. Rahner, cited in Hermann, "Total Humanism," p. 163.

22. A possible exception is Shaull, who interprets the phrase in a strictly temporal sense: "*in* but not *of* the established order . . ."; cf. his "Christian Faith as Scandal in a Technocratic World," *New Theology No. 6*, p. 132. Nor does this appear to be true for van Buren's ethicized version of Christianity's social vision, though his apparent reluctance to identify this vision too closely with secular particulars leaves open the theoretical possibility of a less than total commitment to specific programs of revolutionary change.

23. Rahner, cited in Hermann, "Total Humanism," pp. 168–169.

24. *Ibid.*, pp. 169–170.

25. Metz, cited in Hermann, "Total Humanism," pp. 171–172.

26. The argument of such Marxist humanists as Marcuse is, according to Weissman, that "there is a difference between remaining in the universe of possibilities and saying 'yes' to this particular secular world"; Weissman, "New Left Man," pp. 34, 37.

27. Jürgen Moltmann, "Hope Without Faith: An Eschatological Humanism Without God," in *Is God Dead?* ed. Metz, p. 32.

28. Rahner, in Hermann, p. 162; cf. Karl Rahner, "Christian Humanism," *Journal of Ecumenical Studies*, 4:3 (summer, 1967), pp. 369–384.

29. Rahner, in Hermann, p. 168.

30. The observation and distinctions (*Dasein* and *Vorhandenheit*) are Heidegger's, but they correspond to Ryle's analysis and critique of the category-mistake implicit in the Cartesian (and Platonic) myth of the "ghost in the machine"; cf. *The Concept of Mind* (London, 1949).

31. Moltmann, *Theology of Hope*, p. 92.

32. Shaull, "Revolution," p. 234; cf. Harvey Cox, "The Marxist-Christian Dialogue: What Next?" in *Marxism and Christianity*, ed. Herbert Aptheker (New York, 1968), p. 28.

33. It could be argued that a strictly ethical, i.e., non-theistic interpretation of "secular Christianity" (Braithwaite, van Buren) dissolves this entire problem. To the extent that this is true, our earlier criticisms return with added force: why does this version of the new theology insist on retaining specifically Christian language and practice? Does it fear that an entirely secularized world would lose the distinctive moral contribution of the Judeo-Christian tradition? For a criticism of this ethicist approach to secular theology, cf. MacIntyre, "The Debate About God," pp. 28, 29, 53.

34. Cox, "Marxist-Christian Dialogue," p. 28.

35. Shaull, "Revolution," p. 234.

36. Moltmann, "Hope Without Faith," p. 37.

37. Cf. Leslie Dewart's discussion of this problem (based on a set of distinctions taken from Henri de Lubac), *The Future of Belief* (New York, 1966), pp. 52 ff.

38. Moltmann, "Hope Without Faith," pp. 30–31.

39. This argument is presented by Schubert Ogden, "The Christian Proclamation of God to Men of the So-Called 'Atheistic Age,' " in *Is God Dead?* ed. Metz, pp. 93–96.

40. *Ibid.*, pp. 94–95; cf. also Schubert Ogden, *The Reality of God* (New York, 1966), p. 145, where Ogden finds another source of ontological support for this new metaphysics of God in Heidegger's "existential ontology." Heidegger suggests a conception of God's "eternity" as "a more primal and 'infinite' temporality," rather than an eternal "presence" of Being (cf. Martin Heidegger, *Being and Time* [New York, 1962], p. 499, n. xiii).

41. Cf. Carl Braaten, "Toward a Theology of Hope," *New Theology No. 5*,

pp. 108–109; Ogden, *Reality of God*, p. 153; Moltmann, *Theology of Hope*, p. 110, n. 1: "If . . . the 'historic acts by which Jahweh founded the community were absolute', then this surely means that . . . they overreach their temporal transience and move into the future — it does not mean absoluteness in the sense of intransience."

42. Thus Ogden, "Christian Proclamation," p. 94.

43. Ogden, *Reality of God*, p. 157.

44. This distinction, and the issue involved, is one which Schubert Ogden does not really handle. By making the shift from classical to processive theism, he thinks to have taken care of the atheist's objections. The problem, however, concerns the logical and anthropological significance of "theism" itself. For the radical secularist, with this shift in categories nothing in the essential is changed. *Plus ça change* . . . , etc.

45. Braaten, "Toward a Theology of Hope," p. 109.

46. Although for Marx, "materialism" in its mechanistic or crudely deterministic form is just as much a speculative *ideology*. Like idealism, it accentuates one side of the dialectical relation of "nature" and "consciousness" without referring it back to its prior setting in man's *practical* relation to nature: cf. Marx's First, Second, Fifth and Ninth Theses on Feuerbach.

47. Cf. Moltmann, *Theology of Hope*, pp. 36, 272. This, according to Louis Dupré ("Comment" on George Kline's "Some Critical Comments on Marx's Philosophy," in *Marx and the Western World*, ed. Nicholas Lobkowicz [Notre Dame, Indiana, 1967]), is the proper, "*practical*" meaning of Marx's much misunderstood call for the "abolition" of speculative metaphysics in favor of historical praxis. Marx means only to refuse "any speculation which is a *priori* with respect to *praxis*" (p. 434). Thus, Marx's famous Eleventh Thesis on Feuerbach ("The philosophers have only *interpreted* the world in various ways; the point is, to *change* it") is to be understood as a demand that philosophy answer to *praxis*, not that philosophy be dispensed with in favor of something else.

48. Johannes Metz, "Creative Hope," *New Theology No. 5*, p. 132.

49. *Ibid.*, p. 133.

50. MacIntyre, "The Debate About God," p. 46.

51. *Ibid.*, p. 26.

52. Paul Ricoeur gives a valuable discussion of this specific aspect of the contemporary situation of post-Christian, secular faith in "Religion, Atheism, and Faith," in *Religious Significance of Atheism*, esp. pp. 59, 70, 84, 88.